WATAUGA COUNTY NORTH CAROLINA IN THE CIVIL WAR

MICHAEL C. HARDY

Published by The History Press
Charleston, SC 29403
www.historypress.net

Front cover, top, left to right: William Greene. *Courtesy Sheree Sloop*; Elijah Norris. *Courtesy Wayne Brown*; and Zebulon Baird Vance. *Courtesy North Carolina State Archives*. *Bottom*: Early 1900s reunion. *Courtesy Mike Hartley.*
Back cover, top: Remnants of flags of the Fifty-eighth North Carolina Troops. *Courtesy North Carolina Museum of History*. *Bottom*: Veterans' reunion. *Author's collection*.

First published 2013

Manufactured in the United States

ISBN 978.1.60949.888.7

Library of Congress CIP data applied for.

Contents

Introduction

Jonathan B. Miller, a former member of the Fifty-eighth North Carolina Troops, penned an early twentieth-century book entitled *The Watauga Boys in the Great Civil War.* Miller wanted to write a history of every soldier from Watauga County who had served in the war but lamented that "the lack of information which was to be given by H.A. Davis of the 1st N.C. Cavalry, and Dr. J.B. Phillips of the 37th N.C. infantry, makes it impossible for me to write up the history of those who served in the Eastern Armies… It is hoped that this desired information may be obtained and…given in our second volume." As far as we can ascertain, Miller never completed that second volume. However, thanks to records compiled by the North Carolina Department of Archives and History, we now have accounts of just about every soldier who came from North Carolina and fought "in the Great Civil War."[1]

Like every other project, this present volume rests upon the shoulders of other works. John Preston Arthur, in *A History of Watauga County, North Carolina* (1915) included a chapter, along with scattered little details, about the war and Watauga County. So did Shepherd Monroe Dugger in *War Trails of the Blue Ridge* (1934). Other family and place histories have included bits and pieces of the past. All of those resources have been examined to bring the reader this current volume.

My first interest in the area came in 1995, when I moved to Boone. After much research, I discovered that I have many distant cousins in the area, members of the Councill, Proffitt and Hampton families. In 1995, I began collecting information on the War Between the States and how it connected to Watauga County. This research led to *The Thirty-Seventh North Carolina Troops: Tar Heels in the Army of Northern Virginia* (2003) and *The Fifty-Eighth North Carolina Troops: Tar Heels in the Army of Tennessee* (2011). Most of the men from Watauga County served in one of these two regiments. And then there was *A Short History of Old Watauga County* (2006). This book contained two chapters on the war: one on what happened locally, and the other on the soldiers who marched away. This present volume is an extension of all of those projects.

Research materials for *Watauga County, North Carolina, and the Civil War* have come from a variety of sources: period and postwar newspapers, the papers of Tar Heel governor Zebulon Baird Vance, the correspondence of the North Carolina adjutant general, the Compiled Service Records of Confederate and Union soldiers found in the National Archives, the 1860 Watauga County Federal census, books, family histories and stories told by countless family members over almost two decades. All of these have been gathered, sorted, sifted and woven together to create this work. Though family histories have been extremely helpful in the research, this is not a family history, nor a genealogical study of those who served. While readers may often catch a glimpse of their ancestors, these men and women are part of a large and complex tapestry that covers an entire county, its people and a large scope of events.

Except for a handful of letters, almost all of these accounts are postwar. Watauga County did not have a newspaper in the 1860s. There is an inherent problem with using postwar sources: time seems to alter recollections of events already clouded by the fog of war. Every account included within has been examined and tested for reliability. In some cases, postwar descriptions are all that we have available. A case in point is the raid on Camp Mast in February 1865. The events were apparently first recorded in the 1910s, many decades after the close of the war. Readers must keep that in mind as they peruse these pages. Also, an effort has been made to keep the words of these historical men and women in their original format. While readability might suffer some, these are their voices that are being heard. The structure of the volume also allows room for the voices of both civilians and soldiers. While the first five chapters examine each year of the war as it played out in Watauga County, the sixth chapter looks at the particular experiences of Watauga County soldiers in the Confederate army, where most of them served, at least at some point. While there were Union soldiers from Watauga, unfortunately few of those voices have been preserved for our history. Additional chapters cover the impact of the war on the county and its veterans, as well as the way in which the county has often been misperceived in its role with the war.

A round of thanks is in order. First and foremost, thank you to the people who shared the history of their families. This book is so much the richer, and hopefully these accounts will be preserved for future generations. Evelyn Johnson, late reference librarian at the Watauga County Public Library, helped in a vast number of ways. I regret she passed on and did not live to see this project completed. And to my manuscript readers, Terry Harmon and Elizabeth Baird Hardy, thanks for making this book the best that it can be.

Chapter 1

1861

It is not clear just what caused Sheriff A.J. McBride and a group of others to attempt riding their horses through the Watauga County Courthouse at the annual militia muster in October 1861. It could have been the excitement over the war, or possibly a little too much corn whiskey circulated at the festivities after the muster. Regardless, Clerk of Court Joseph B. Todd, who had just returned from the Confederate army, was forced to brandish his sword, keeping the riders at bay. While musters were often boisterous affairs, the 1861 event also reflected the mood of a populace who saw the new war as an exciting escape and had yet to be proven tragically wrong.[2]

Perhaps Watauga's exuberance could be attributed to the county's youth. Watauga County was just eleven years old when the secession crisis erupted in 1860. The county was formed in 1849, mostly from Ashe County, with smaller portions coming from Wilkes, Caldwell and Yancey Counties. Watauga drew its name from the Watauga River that flowed through the area. Councill's Store, the only sizable hamlet in the new county, was chosen as the county seat and renamed Boone. Legendary explorer Daniel Boone had camped in the area during his numerous hunting forays across the Blue Ridge.

According to the United States census, taken just a year after the county was formed, the population was only 3,400 men, women and children, with 129 slaves. Watauga County was a very rough and rugged place. While there were some valleys where agriculture was practiced, much of the terrain was mountainous. Many families survived by subsistence farming, and the

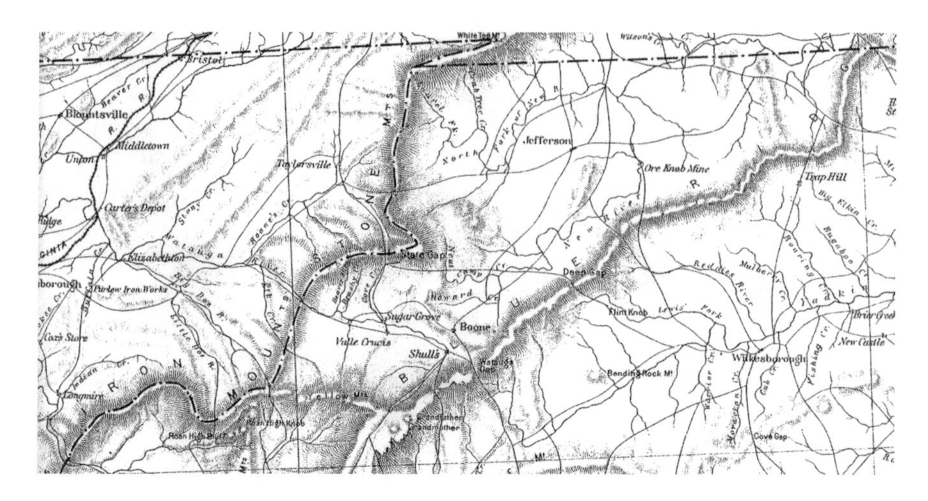

This wartime map depicts Watauga County and surrounding areas in the 1860s. *Author's collection.*

major commodities exported outside county lines were hogs. The fertile valley regions of Cove Creek, Valle Crucis, Meat Camp, Bethel and Mabel attracted most of the farmers. There were a few churches in the county, mostly Baptist and Methodist, with an Episcopal church in Valle Crucis. There were also a few schools and, by 1860, eleven post offices.

Also by 1860, the population had grown to 4,957 people, which included 104 slaves and 32 free persons of color. There were thirty-three schools, with 902 students. The county allotment from the State School Fund was just $401.76, the smallest in North Carolina. Watauga also had the smallest slave population in North Carolina.[3]

Watauga County men went to the polls in August 1860 to elect the next governor of North Carolina. On the ballot was John Pool, an eastern North Carolina planter and lawyer. Pool had been a member of the Whig party before its demise and, in the 1860 election, ran on the Opposition Party ticket. He supported *ad valorem* taxation in which slave owners would be compelled to contribute a more reasonable burden of taxation. Pool's opponent was incumbent John W. Ellis, a Democrat opposed to the *ad valorem* tax but in favor of state-sponsored internal improvements. In the end, local men cast 442 votes for Pool and only 259 for Ellis. However, Ellis won the election statewide.[4]

Of greater importance was the presidential election coming in November. Due to a split in the Democratic Party, there was a wealth of candidates. At a convention in Charleston, South Carolina, in April 1860, the Democratic Party had split over the party's platform. A portion of the party wanted the endorsement of *Dred Scott*, a Supreme Court decision that stated that African Americans were property, not citizens, and that the federal government had no power to regulate slavery in the territories, along with new Congressional legislation protecting slavery in the territories. When this report was not adopted in favor of the "fire-eaters," who advocated immediate secession, they walked out of the convention. A second convention met in Baltimore, Maryland, six weeks later, also ending in turmoil. In the end, the Northern branch of the Democratic Party nominated Illinois senator Stephen Douglas while the Southern branch of the party nominated Vice President John Breckinridge of Kentucky. Joining Douglas and Breckinridge on the ballot was John Bell, a member of the Constitutional Union Party.

Election Day was Tuesday, November 6. Watauga County men cast 469 votes: 322 for Bell, 147 for Breckinridge and none for Douglas. Statewide, Breckinridge won the election with 48,538 votes compared with 44,900 for Bell and 2,701 for Douglas. The winner of the national election, Republican Abraham Lincoln, was not even on the ballot in North Carolina. Many in the Deep South were concerned over the election of a Republican president. The recently created Republican Party advocated high tariffs on imported goods, including cotton shipped from the South. The money generated by these tariffs would support internal improvements in the Northern states. Also advocated was a national bank, something that had been opposed by Southerners for generations. Most troubling was the desire to close slavery to new territories considering statehood, a position that had helped form the Republican Party just a few years earlier. Following Lincoln's election, the states in the Deep South began to hold conventions, meetings to take them out of the Union. South Carolina seceded on December 20, 1861, followed by Mississippi, Florida, Alabama, Georgia, Louisiana and Texas.

The governor of North Carolina in 1860 was John Ellis, who, while a secessionist, still agreed with Senator William A. Graham that "the necessity for revolution does not yet exist." However, Ellis was clear when he wrote in October 1860 that the use of military force by the United States government "against one of the southern states *would* present an emergency demanding prompt and decided action on our part. It can but be manifest that a blow thus aimed at one of the southern States would involve the whole country in civil war." Nevertheless, it was Ellis in November 1860 who proposed meeting with the states that "identified with us in interest and in the wrongs we have suffered," while at the same time proposing the reorganization of the militia and a convention of the people in North Carolina. All across the state, meetings that advocated a pro-Union stance, or a pro-Southern, Confederate stance, rapidly began occurring. Although there is no surviving record of such a meeting in Watauga County, meetings did occur in Caldwell County in December 1860.[5]

On January 29, the General Assembly passed legislation that called for the men of the state to gather on February 28 and vote on the question of calling a convention, while at the same time electing 120 delegates. It is not clear what level of campaigning took place in Watauga County. John B. Palmer, a recent arrival to the area who owned a large estate along the Linville River, chronicled in August 1865 that he "became a candidate…for a State Convention and in campaigning…took strong and decided grounds against secession and counseled the people to vote against the convention scheme." Palmer's exact role is unclear, as his lands along the Linville River became a part of Mitchell County in early 1861. When the votes were tallied, 536 in Watauga were against calling a convention, while 72 voted in favor. Statewide, the vote was closer: 47,322 votes against calling the convention, with 46,672 for the convention, a margin of just 650 votes. Elected to represent Watauga County, had the convention been called, was James W. Councill, son of Jordan Councill Jr. James W. Councill lived in Boone and was a blacksmith, along with being a justice of the peace. According to the census, he owned three slaves.[6]

People all across the state continued to watch and wait. The next two months were tense, but bit by bit, the attitudes of North Carolinians toward disunion were gradually transformed. The first change occurred when a peace conference assembled in Washington, D.C., failed to achieve any results on February 27, 1861. A week later, Lincoln delivered his inaugural address, which also included his first statements regarding the crisis at hand. His comments were rather vague: a secessionist would have labeled the address as belligerent while a Unionist would have believed it conciliatory. Added to the mix were the words pouring forth from North Carolina's own "fire-eaters," including western North Carolinians Thomas Clingman and William W. Avery. Clingman was a United States senator from Buncombe County, and Avery was a state politician from Burke County. Both campaigned for immediate secession. In early April 1861, Lincoln ordered troops to embark toward Fort Sumter in Charleston, South Carolina. The troops were to reinforce the small Federal garrison there. Confederate forces surrounding the fort on land viewed this as a hostile act; on the morning of April 12, before the troops could be unloaded, the Confederates opened fire. The fort capitulated three days later. Three days after that, Lincoln declared that an insurrection existed and requested that the states call up 75,000 militia. North Carolina's quota was 1,500 men. "Your dispatch is received," Governor Ellis telegraphed back, "and if genuine, which its extraordinary character leads me to doubt, I have to say in reply, that I regard the levy of troops made by the administration for the purpose of subjugating the states of the South, as in violation of the Constitution, and as a gross usurpation of power. I can be no party to this violation of the laws of the country and to this war upon liberties of a free people. You can get no troops from North Carolina." Ellis ordered the seizure of the forts along the coast, the arsenal in Fayetteville and the mint in Charlotte. On May 1, the General Assembly met, with the house unanimously passing a bill calling for an election of 120 delegates on May 13 and then a convention to meet in Raleigh on May 20. The Senate then passed the same bill, with three dissenting votes.[7]

Colonel John B. Palmer of the Fifty-eighth North Carolina Troops originally campaigned against secession. *From Clark's* North Carolina Troops.

It is unclear if there was a contest in Watauga County, or if James W. Councill ran unopposed. In any case, he was elected to represent the county in the convention in Raleigh. On May 20, the convention passed an ordinance of secession, followed by an ordinance ratifying the Provisional Constitution of the Confederate States of America. The secession ordinance was signed by all 120 delegates the next day.

Like those in many counties, Watauga County men had not waited for the conventioneers to act. Early in the month of May, a group of fifty men met and responded to the call for volunteers "to meet and resist the Invasion of our Enemies." These volunteers pledged "Our Lives, our Properties, and our Sacred Honors to defend the Rights[,] Institutions and Honor of our County, State, and our Common Country, the Confederate States of

America." William Y. Farthing was elected captain and was granted the authority to call the company together when he felt it necessary. The uniform of the company was "Blue mixed Homespun Pants with Black Stripes and common Mountain Hunting Shirt trimmed with brass buttons, the collar & pockets trimmed with Black, and the Parade Coat to be of the same material made according to Army regulations, of the State." There were fifty-one names on the list, and all but one went on to serve in the Confederate army.[8]

That same month, George N. Folk, a middle-class lawyer who owned two slaves and was Watauga County's representative in the General Assembly, returned to Boone to recruit his own company. Folk was from Virginia and married to Elizabeth Councill, a sister of James W. Councill. On April 17, Folk had written from Asheville to Governor Ellis, tendering his "resignation as a member of the legislature." Folk was back in Boone on May 11, with permission to raise a company. According to Harvey Davis, "after a some-what firey speech by…Folk…in which the speaker dwelt at large on the attempt of the North to dominate the South and abrogate her rights under the Constitution, [a] call was made for volunteers. The writer was requested to carry and beat the brass drum after which those who wished to volunteer was requested to march." Watauga County had no newspaper at this time, and it is unlikely that printed posters were circulated to draw attention to the fact that Folk was organizing a company. Word obviously was passed from person to person. Recruits came from all over the county, although the majority came from the Boone, Meat Camp and Blue Ridge Districts. And there were recruits of all ages. Daniel Moretz was a forty-three-year-old millwright who served until November 20, 1862, when he was discharged for "old age." William R. Lewis was but seventeen. The average age was almost twenty-eight years old. About half were married. Folk was elected captain. John C. Blair and Joseph B. Todd were first lieutenants. James W. Councill, who was "Absent attending N.C. state convention," was elected second lieutenant. Most of the company were middle class, with only Councill in the upper-class bracket. A few, like nineteen-year-old Isaac Green, were day laborers; Green had only forty-four dollars in personal property and no land.[9]

Harvey Davis goes on in his diary to tell that Folk's company spent four weeks in Boone after volunteering. Amongst the daily drill, the company of men "were invited and partook of several public banquets, set by the hospitable citizens of the county, among which we might name one at Col. Jonathan Hortons & one at John Moretz…We passed the time very enjoyably with the local citizens." On June 8, the men rode out of Boone, "Bidding

General Assemblyman George N. Folk served as captain, Company D, of the first North Carolina Cavalry and, later, as colonel of the Sixth North Carolina Cavalry. *From Clark's* North Carolina Troops.

good by to the hosts of citizens who had assembled to see the first soldiers leave" the county. Davis recalled that one of the new cavalrymen, when telling his wife goodbye, "told her to take care of her self, when she burst into a hearty laugh, remarking I think it is you, who should be careful of your self." Hattie Green recalled that her aunt Susan Farthing was standing with her boyfriend, watching the soldiers march by. Susan recalled that "he just stepped out from the crowd and told her goodbye and then caught up with" the new soldiers. Folk led his company, "The Watauga Rangers," to Valle Crucis the first day, camping at Henry Taylor's. The second day they made it to Cranberry and, by June 13, were in Asheville. The Rangers became Company D, First North Carolina Cavalry.[10]

As Folk left Watauga County, he had "ten or fifteen free negros to tend on them." These men and boys served as camp cooks and laborers. Also in tow were two free persons of color, Franklin and William Henry Cozzens. Apparently, Folk had impressed the brothers into service as camp servants and lodged them in the jail in Boone. When the company left Boone, the brothers went to Asheville. Mark Holtsclaw, who had represented the county in the General Assembly in 1858, wrote to Governor Ellis on June 17,

1861, asking the governor to order the brothers released. "[O]ne of them [Franklin] had a small family and a little farm," Holtsclaw wrote, "the other was a young man 16 or 17 years old helping his aged father maintain a large family…Both under good Caracter and would pass for whitemen tho their father says tha are desendants of the portigee [Portuguese]." The Cozzens brothers were back at home by August 1861, when Holtsclaw again wrote to the authorities in Raleigh asking for a letter stating that, since the Cozzens brothers were free persons of color, they were not bound to perform state service: Captain Folk "is threatening to send for the boys and force them back." The 1860 census shows just thirty-two free persons of color in the entire county. Folk's collection of "ten or fifteen negros" must have included all of the young men, none of whom would have been liable for military service since they were not white.[11]

The loss of so many men, gone from the community on what was perceived as some grand adventure, did not seem to dampen the mood of the majority. An estimated 650 local citizens gathered "for the last time to celebrate the anniversary of the Fourth of July." The crowd heard speeches by "Messrs. Hodge, Col. J. Horton, and H.M. Stokes, upon the impending crisis; and they were attentively heard by the large audience and much applauded, for the firm and patriotic sentiments uttered upon the occasion." The militia then drilled for two hours, before sitting down to a dinner prepared by members of the Bradley, Potter, Triplett and other families. Joel Waters even composed some original verse for the day:

For forty years, now past and gone,
We bore the tyrant's red;
We wanted nothing but our own,
Nor thirsted for their blood.
We strove for peace in every way,
Because we thought it right—
But since that peaceful day is gone,
We're now resolved to fight.[12]

The first major battle of the war was fought July 21, 1861, on the plains of Manassas, along Bull Run, not far from Washington City. It was a Confederate victory. Many felt that had the Confederate army continued to advance to take the Federal capital, the war would have ended. In reality, the Federal loss at Manassas stiffened the resolve of the Federal populace. It also proved to everyone that this would not be a short war. More troops would be needed from North Carolina, and the other Southern states, to sustain the war effort.

Governor Ellis died of tuberculosis on July 7, 1861, and was replaced by Henry T. Clark, Speaker of the North Carolina Senate. Following the battle of Manassas, the Confederate congress authorized the president to call up to 400,000 more volunteers. Prior to his death, it had fallen to Ellis to raise more troops, and Watauga County men once again answered the call. Farmer and former state legislator Jonathan Horton set about to raise one of those companies. Horton was fifty-five years old and, at least in local terms, a prosperous farmer and slave owner. He lived in the Boone district, and the majority of his recruits came from the Boone and Blue Ridge districts. The new company chose to call themselves the "Watauga Marksmen," and, on September 14, 1861, ninety-three of them volunteered for service. They elected Horton captain, Jordan Cook first lieutenant, Calvin Carlton second lieutenant and Andrew J. Critcher third lieutenant. Joining the men that day in Horton's company were Franklin and William Henry Cozzens. Instead of being kidnapped to serve as camp laborers, this time the brothers willingly volunteered to serve. William, the younger brother, served as a teamster for much of the war and was captured in April 1865. He later moved to Yancey County. His brother Franklin was killed in the fighting at Second Manassas, Virginia, in August 1862, leaving a wife and small child back in Watauga County. William Y. Farthing organized the second company that month. He was a forty-nine-year-old, middle-class farmer living in the Beaver Dam district. Paul Farthing was elected first lieutenant; William F. Shull, second lieutenant; and Isaac Wilson, third lieutenant. This group of men, primarily from the Beaver Dam, Valle Crucis and Cove Creek districts, chose to call themselves the "Watauga Minute Men." Though evidence is sparse, it appears that the Watauga Minute Men were presented a flag before departing for the war, probably by a group of local ladies. The flag bore the inscription "Watauga Minute Men" and was carried by David C. Dugger. Writing in 1898, Dugger was unsure what had happened to the banner, believing that it had been captured in May 1862. The Watauga Marksmen and the Watauga Minute Men were mustered into the Thirty-seventh North Carolina Troops on November 20, 1861.[13]

There were rumors of incursions and disloyalty to the Confederacy as early as August 1861. First came a story in which east Tennessee "tories" raided into Watauga County, "abducting several citizens" and holding "the persons taken as hostages for the safety of Nelson." The validity of the story remains unclear. "Nelson" was most likely Thomas A.R. Nelson, a congressman from Jonesborough, Tennessee. Elected for a second term in Congress in 1861, Nelson was on his way to Washington, D.C., to take his seat when he was arrested and imprisoned in Richmond. A couple of weeks later came a newspaper report, widely distributed, of a group of "Fifty to one hundred Tennesseeans and Wataugans" crossing over into Watauga County "trying to arouse those people against the Southern movements." Cavalry had been dispatched to the area "to bring them back." It was the advice of the newspaper that North Carolina should "be on her guard, and let her authorities hang or shoot every tory and Yankee they may lay their hands upon. If they make any more demonstrations in Watauga, the farmers should rise en masse to suppress them." The Raleigh *Standard* transmitted more information on the mobs that roamed through eastern Tennessee, adding "that the militia of Ashe, Watauga and other counties on the western line" of North Carolina "turned out in such numbers to meet the Lincolnites of East Tennessee." There is probably some validity to the newspaper articles. Barzilla McBride, serving in the First Cavalry, wrote home to his brothers and sisters on August 25, 1861: "I was sorry to hear that them tories was creating so much excitement if our Regiment was up there in N.C. we could soon clear them out."[14]

The war came close to home when, on the night of November 8, a group of Unionists led by Carter County, Tennessee resident Reverend William B. Carter burned, or attempted to burn, several bridges along the East Tennessee and Georgia and the East Tennessee and Virginia railroads. These lines were vital links for transporting troops, munitions and foodstuffs from the Deep South into Virginia. Only four of the nine targeted bridges were burned, and the support of Federal troops under the command of General William T. Sherman in eastern Kentucky failed to materialize. Dozens of suspected Unionists were arrested and jailed, and several were hanged. While there is no evidence that Watauga County men were involved, the Northern press claimed that the bridge burners "were aided by mountaineers from Watauga county, North Carolina, adjacent." Yet another article in a Massachusetts newspaper claimed that the plot originated in Watauga County, with men from east Tennessee helping.[15]

With the events in August and November, there were some who appeared to doubt the loyalty of the people in Watauga County. This prompted a citizen of Caldwell County, possibly Walter W. Lenoir, to write an article entitled "The Loyalty of Watauga County Vindicated." A Richmond newspaper article about the bridge burners stated that five hundred men from Watauga had crossed over the line and joined the Unionists. The defender of Watauga explained that the county already had three companies in Confederate service and that "no portion of the Southern people are represented by a braver, hardier, or more patriotic band of men.

> *They are all marks men, accustomed to take a fine sight upon their objects, and death is sure to follow the report of their rifles. A large portion of them have left their farms and young families in the care of the old folks, and gone to distant and sickly portions of the republic, determined to drive back the Northern vandals, or perish in the attempt. While lately at the house of Amos Green, a citizen of Watauga...he told me that four of his five sons were in the army, and his wife joining in said, that if necessary, the last one should go, and the women would do the work themselves...The imaginary line dividing Watauga from East Tennessee is a real line of division in sentiment between her people and the traitors of that disaffected region. And I am happy to be able to state, from personal knowledge, that they are as heartily united in the cause of the south as any people in the Confederacy.*[16]

As 1861 drew to a close, almost three hundred Watauga County men were away fighting the war or at least struggling to stay warm in a camp in eastern North Carolina or Virginia. As the events of August 1861 showed, the war was not that far from old Watauga, and there would soon be far more serious matters than horses in the courthouse to concern its citizens.

Chapter 2

1862

While in 1861 the Confederate forces were victorious at places like Fort Sumter, South Carolina; Manassas, Virginia; and Wilson's Creek, Missouri, the next year brought a series of defeats. The battle of Mill Springs, Kentucky, was won by Federal forces in January 1862. Fort Donelson, Tennessee, fell to Union forces in February, and the battles of Pea Ridge, Arkansas, and Shiloh, Tennessee, were also Confederate losses.

Confederate president Jefferson Davis was facing a manpower shortage. Many men in the Confederate army had enlisted to serve for one year, and as the first signs of spring spread across the countryside, those periods of enlistment were set to expire. As early as December 1861, there had been talk of passing a conscription law. Instead of passing that law, the Confederate Congress passed the Furlough and Bounty Act in late December 1861. All of the men who voluntarily reenlisted for the war received a fifty-dollar bounty and a furlough home. When it became apparent that voluntary reenlistments would fall woefully short, Jefferson Davis submitted legislation to Congress that required all able-bodied, white males between the ages of eighteen and thirty-five to enlist in the army for three years or the war. The bill passed on April 16 and became known as the Conscription Act. A second act passed on April 21, exempting from military service "Confederate and State legislative, executive and judicial officials and their clerks and employees; ferrymen, pilots and all engaged in river and railroad transportation work; employees in iron mines, foundries and furnaces; telegraph operators, ministers; printers, educators; hospital employees; druggists; and certain employees in wool and cotton mills." Further exemptions were later allowed for men who made salt or those who owned more than twenty slaves.

Men already in the army were forced to "volunteer" for three years or the war. A provision allowed the regiments in the field to reorganize and to elect new officers. For some men, this was a chance to replace strict disciplinarians with less stringent leaders. No mass turnover took place in the Thirty-seventh, but Second Lieutenant David J. Green and First Lieutenant Paul Farthing were both defeated for reelection. Many of the rank and file were against the Conscription Act. "There is good deal of flusteration in the Ridgment at this time," wrote Bennett Smith on April 17, 1862, "cosed by the brutish laws they hav past they have forst awl the 12 months boys during the war or two years I think it is a mean trick I fear our leading men is a corupt body of men."[17]

A grace period was given to allow men not already in the army to volunteer for service. These volunteers were often promised a bounty, usually fifty dollars, and were permitted to join whatever company they chose, allowing them to serve with family and acquaintances. Those who waited were conscripted and placed in any regiment that might need them. Once again, with a lack of printing resources, the news was spread via word of mouth. Even though as a minister he was exempt, Reverend Drewey Harmon, the former pastor of Cove Creek Baptist Church and the register of deeds, received permission to recruit a company on May 13. The men in Harmon's company came primarily from the Laurel Creek, Cove Creek and Valle Crucis districts, with a few from the Meat Camp, Boone, Blue Ridge and Beaver Dam districts. The average age was twenty-four years old, but there were many who were under twenty or over thirty. Harmon was elected captain on June 27. Also elected that day were Benjamin Baird, first lieutenant; William Mast, second lieutenant; and William Howington, third lieutenant. Howington had previously served in the First Cavalry. Mast had recently returned from a failed relocation trip to Texas.[18]

Forty-eight-year-old farmer William Miller was also working on raising a company. Most of Miller's men came from Cove Creek and Meat Camp districts, with a few from Valle Crucis and Boone districts. The average age was twenty-five years old. Miller was a veteran. He had served in forces that helped with the Cherokee removal in 1836 and in the Mexican-American War a decade later. When the Civil War broke out, he volunteered in May 1861 in the First Cavalry until February 1862, when he was discharged by reason of a "broken down constitution." Also elected to help with command was William M. Hodges, first lieutenant; Jordan C. McGee, second

John A. Mast, pictured with his wife, Martha Moore Mast, was thirty-two years old when he joined Company D, Fifty-eighth North Carolina Troops. *Courtesy Terry Harmon.*

lieutenant; and James H. Horton, third lieutenant. Miller's company was known as the Watauga Troopers.[19]

Both Harmon's and Miller's companies journeyed to Mitchell County and camped out on the grounds of John B. Palmer's Grasslands estate. On July 29, 1862, both companies were mustered into Confederate service, becoming part of the Fifty-eighth North Carolina Troops. Harmon's company was designated Company D, and Miller's command became Company I. Palmer was elected colonel of the regiment. Wesley W. Presnell, a member of Company D, recalled after the war that the new soldiers spent their first night in the service in the loft of a barn owned by James Blair, a spot also known as the Old Eggers Place. Instead of heading east, the Fifty-eighth Regiment turned west and was assigned to the Army of Tennessee.[20]

There was a third company from Watauga County in the Fifty-eighth Regiment. Company M was organized on September 26, 1862, with men from Watauga and Ashe Counties. The regiment was under the command of Captain Jonathan L. Phillips, with George Hopkins, first lieutenant; John R. Norris, second lieutenant; and Thomas Ray, third lieutenant. Almost all of the enlisted men within this company were conscripts, men forced into the army against their will. Many of these men or boys came from middle-class families. One, James C. Lewis, even came from a slave-holding family. At the same time, some of the poorest men in Watauga County were members of this company. The men primarily came from the Cove Creek, Meat Camp and Blue Ridge districts. Almost every enlisted man within this company later deserted, many hiding out in the mountains for the duration of the war.[21]

Conscription tore the mountain communities apart. Many who were lukewarm to the idea of a Southern Confederacy were compelled to fight for the new nation. And many more who were indifferent were forced into hiding, trying to avoid military service. William C. Baird was trying to get through the lines when he was caught by the home guard. He escaped and was compelled to hide in a rock house not far from his home during the war. Similarly, George W. Eggers took to "scouting," trying to avoid the recruiters from both armies. Once, while he was hiding upstairs in his home, his wife, Lucinda, "took a piece of burning chestnut bark from the fireplace and gave one soldier a whack with it as he was climbing the ladder." On another occasion, Eggers was concealed beneath the floor at a neighbor's house. He had a bad cough, and he "said it liked to killed him trying to hold back his cough." The experiences of Baird and Eggers were typical of the time.[22]

There were a few local men who were truly Unionists, and to avoid conscription and service in the Confederate army, they chose to cross over the mountains and at least reach the safety of Union lines. Shepherd Dugger recalled that, "One evening in August…eight young men gathered in our cabin…With tearful eyes and affected voices they bade us good-bye and stepped out into the darkness." Even though their family was one of the largest slaveholding households in Watauga County, several members of the Banner family chose to cross over the mountain that August in 1862. Oliver, Columbus, Newton and Henry Banner all joined the Fourth Tennessee Cavalry on August 8, 1862, at Cumberland Gap. Newton supposedly told the officer in charge that "he wanted to fight and if he did not take him in this army, he would join the other side." Newton then took the oath on the corner of three states: Kentucky, Tennessee and Virginia.[23]

Another interesting story concerning conscription evasion is that of the Blalocks, even though it is hard to discern fact from fiction. William M. "Keith" Blalock and his wife, Malinda Pritchard, lived in Coffey's Gap, in the Blue Ridge District of Watauga County. When the Conscription Act became a reality, but before its enforcement, Blalock chose to voluntarily enlist in the Confederate army, joining Company F, Twenty-sixth North Carolina Troops, on March 20, 1862. Enlisting that same day was Samuel Blalock, reportedly Keith's younger brother. "Sam" was really his wife, Malinda. She had cut off her hair and donned men's clothing, disguising her gender to be near her husband. It is unclear if Keith was originally part of this ruse. Regardless, both were mustered into the Confederate army. The Twenty-sixth North Carolina was stationed near Kinston during this time. According to her service record, Malinda's "disguise was never penetrated. She drilled and did the duties of a soldier as any other member of the company, and was very adept at learning the manual and drill." According to a postwar account, she "wore a private's uniform and tented and messed with Keith. She watched the men 'when they went in swimming'...but never went in herself." Early Watauga County historian John Preston Arthur wrote, "Keith was a Union man and joined only to avoid conscription and in the hope that opportunity might offer for him to desert to the Union lines." Deciding after a month that he had had enough of army life, Keith went into the swamp and rubbed down with poison sumac. He presented himself to the regimental surgeon and was discharged on April 20, 1862, by reason of "hernia" and "poison from sumac." Not wishing to remain in the army without Keith, Malinda revealed her secret to her captain, who then took her to the colonel, Zebulon B. Vance. Malinda was discharged, and the couple returned to the mountains. Contemporary information about the duo is sparse, taken mostly from the compiled service record and an article that appeared in the *Western Democrat* in May 1862. The editor considered the whole situation a "novel incident. A short time ago some recruits came from Caldwell county, among them a man named Blaylew [*sic*]...Week before last Blaylew got his

Keith and Malinda Blalock both served in the Twenty-sixth North Carolina Troops and as pilots on a local underground railroad; Keith later enlisted with the Tenth Michigan Cavalry. *Courtesy Avery County Historical Museum.*

discharge, and immediately another soldier applied for a discharge, saying that he (or she) was the lawful wife of Blaylew…The boys were sorry to part with such a good soldier, but they are unable to determine which she loved best, Blaylew or the Confederacy; but it was unanimously voted that Mrs. Blaylew is 'some punkins.'" The accounts of the Blalocks leave many questions. If Blalock was truly a Union man, then he could have crossed over the mountain like the Banners did and joined the Union army. Or, upon arriving at Kinston, he could have attempted to reach the Union army, less than forty miles away. Instead of truly being a "Union man," Blalock was more likely a dissident. He did not officially join the Union army until mid-1864 and, even then, never left the area. According to his pension record, his officers questioned many of his actions, even going so far as to state that Blalock might have been a deserter from the Union army at times.[24]

The mass exodus of men from the county created problems for the militia. Each county in North Carolina constituted a militia regiment.

Prior to the war, Watauga County was the 107th Regiment, North Carolina Militia. However, the state reorganized the militia in September 1861, and the county was re-designated as the 98th Regiment, North Carolina Militia. William Horton was appointed colonel in March 1862. The county was divided up into militia districts: Shoney Haw, Soda Hill, Rotherwood, Blue Ridge, Watauga, Beaver Dam, Cove Creek, Laurel Hill and Boone. Each district had a captain and first and second lieutenants. Militia law stated that all free white males between the ages of eighteen and forty-five were members of a county's militia. They were required to furnish themselves with long arms, shot pouches and powder horns. The individual companies were to meet twice a year for drill, and the entire regiment was to meet once a year for drill. The regimental muster ground was located to the east of Boone, and the annual muster was slated to take place on the second Saturday of October. Like the weeks when court was in secession, the annual militia muster was a social affair. Following drill, a large banquet was often laid. Jugs of some of Watauga County's finest distilled apples and corn flowed freely.[25]

With the Conscription Act of April 1862 taking all white males between the ages of eighteen and thirty-five, the militia was left in shambles. Militia officers were considered government employees and were exempt from the draft. A steady stream of correspondence flowed between the adjutant general's office in Raleigh and Watauga County. Dr. George Evans of Valle Crucis had written the adjutant general in July 1862. Apparently, William Horton was trying to force Evans to become surgeon of the militia regiment, which, according to the adjutant general's office, Horton could not do. Some former militia officers had evidently written the adjutant general in August, wanting to know if they could get out of the army. The reply was that they "are not entitled to be discharged because they held commissions." John Ward wrote the adjutant general in October, wanting to know if he, the sergeant major of the regiment, was exempt from the Conscription Act. The answer was no, the noncommissioned officers were not exempt.[26]

One of the roles of the militia was to round up those who were absent without leave or deserters. On September 18, Governor Vance issued a proclamation that asked citizens who were attempting to organize resistance to the Conscription Act to submit to the law. The next day, the adjutant general wrote to Colonel Horton in Boone, enclosing a copy of the governor's proclamation and ordering Horton to call out the militia to blockade the mountain passes and "arrest all deserting Conscripts as well as those…who have failed to report themselves to Camp." The adjutant general added that the impending arrest of "those lawless men on Stone Mountain will be brought to their better judgement [*sic*]." Stone Mountain is located on the border separating Watauga County from Tennessee.[27]

In October, the adjutant general, under orders from the governor, wrote to Colonel Horton, asking him to arrest deserters from the Thirty-seventh Regiment. These included Stephen Broyhill, James Carroll, William Church and Jordan S. Councill from Company B and Lewis Orrant, David Brewer, J. Anderson Pritchard, Andrew Baird, Nathaniel Shull, William Green, George Younce, Cicero Harmon, James Brewer, Samuel Clark, Britton South, Sherman Swift, Simon Shull, William Harden and Joseph Howington of Company E. Some of these men returned voluntarily, and some, like Samuel Clark, are listed as having been apprehended. Others, like Stephen Broyhill, who deserted in March 1862, evaded authorities for the rest of the war. Apparently, some militia officers did not work fast enough for the government. The adjutant general wrote to Aaron Von Cannon, captain of the Valle Crucis company, in November 1862, stating that Colonel Horton "reported to this Office that you have failed to arrest conscripts in your district. You are herby directed to arrest these immediately and forward them to Camp Holmes." Maybe this was due to Von Cannon's divided loyalties, as the militia officer's register later described him as having "Gone to the Enemy."[28]

There were yet other problems with the Ninety-eighth Regiment, North Carolina Militia. In an election in December 1862 for the position of lieutenant colonel, so few votes were cast that the adjutant general ruled that the position would remain vacant. Jonathan L. Phillips held the post on May 17, 1862, but volunteered for service and was elected captain of Company M, Fifty-eighth Regiment on September 26, 1862. A letter was also addressed to Major Joseph Matherson of the Ninety-eighth Regiment in December, returning commissions for militia officers except for four men. These men were liable for conscription and could no longer serve in the militia.[29]

Watauga County voters went to the polls again in September 1862 to elect a new governor. Henry T. Clark, who was elevated to the position of governor upon Ellis's death, chose not to seek election. On the ballot instead was William Johnston, a railroad president from Charlotte and a member of the Confederate Party. Running against him on the Conservative platform was Colonel Zebulon B. Vance, a Buncombe County native. The Confederate Party members wholeheartedly supported Jefferson Davis's policies and were willing to suppress their convictions regarding states' rights for the greater

Buncombe County native Zebulon Baird Vance served as colonel of the Twenty-sixth North Carolina Troops and then as North Carolina's wartime governor, receiving many letters from Watauga County men about the conditions of the war in the mountains. *Courtesy North Carolina Museum of History.*

Confederate cause. Many members of the Conservative Party were former conditional Unionists, supporters of states' rights, and often opposed Davis and the government when they infringed on those rights. Vance handily won the election, gaining 54,423 votes to Johnston's 20,448. In Watauga, only 62 votes were cast for Johnston, while Vance earned 423.[30]

As 1862 drew to a close, the heartache of war had reached many a cabin door. Local men, primarily in the Thirty-seventh Regiment, had fought in some of the hardest battles of the war up to that date. These included Hanover Court House, Gaines Mill, Cedar Mountain, Second Manassas and Fredericksburg in Virginia, along with Harpers Ferry, Sharpsburg (Antietam) and Falling Waters in Maryland. In 1862, the two Watauga County companies in the Thirty-seventh Regiment lost twenty-four killed or mortally wounded on the battlefield and thirty who died of disease. In comparison, Company D, First Cavalry, lost one killed and five to disease, while the Watauga companies of the Fifty-eighth Regiment lost two killed and two who died of disease. The losses in the field, along with the desolation felt at home, continued to grow after 1862.

Chapter 3

1863

A serious factor throughout the war was the weather. Not only did adverse conditions hamper the movements of troops and supplies, but they also affected the people back home. Toward the later part of 1862, a drought besieged much of western North Carolina. The estimated crop production, already diminished by the absence of men serving in the army, was reduced by at least another one-third. Added to this was the report of snow in the mountains of western North Carolina on October 25, 1862. It was a long winter, and conditions did not improve throughout the next year. John Preston Arthur chronicled, "There was frost in every month" in 1863. Such harsh circumstances, coupled with the drought of 1862, exacerbated the anxiety among the civilian population.[31]

Despite the meteorological challenges, local citizens were still trying to increase efforts to care for their own soldiers. On January 7, 1863, the *Weekly Standard* from Raleigh reported the items that had been collected for the soldiers and sent from Watauga County. These donations included "36 blankets, 2 coats, 8 pr drawers, 4 shirts, 33 pr socks, 5 quilts, 4 pr pants, [and] 8 vests." Soldiers often wrote to their loved ones in Watauga County, asking that clothes and foodstuffs be sent to the front. Leah Adams Dougherty recalled later in life, "I was called out of bed any hour of the night to cook and pack a knapsack with three-day rations for my soldier brothers, and for men who were on furlough or returning to the front."[32]

Dougherty also recalled melting pewter plates for bullets, gathering sourwood leaves to make gray dye for military clothes and making envelopes for neighbors: "I saved every bit of wrapping paper and smoothed it out very carefully; then I'd cut it into shape and glue it together with white of an egg…Sometimes letters would be written on rhododendron leaves." She helped her mother, Betsy Adams, work flax into thread, which was then woven into linen shirts. At the same time, the family also wove and dyed cloth for blankets. "Confederate money was worth nothing. Even if it had been, there was nothing to buy. We made coffee from parched wheat and rye. We had no meat, nor milk, nor sugar."[33]

Salt was another serious concern. Local residents required salt to preserve the meat—primarily pork—that sustained them throughout the long winters. The government often appointed a salt agent responsible for procuring salt and distributing it to needy families loyal to the Confederacy. Those families who had relations who were hiding out, or who were known to have crossed over the mountain and joined the Union army, were left to fend for themselves. In Madison County, this led to the salt raid in Marshall and the Shelton Laurel Massacre in January 1863. While the identity of the salt agent for Watauga County is not known, family tradition has it that Joseph H. Mast led an expedition to the salt works in Saltville, Virginia, to procure the vital commodity.[34]

Conditions across the state took a turn for the worse in February 1863. Local militia engaged a group of draft dodgers in a Yadkin County schoolhouse. Four men were killed, including two members of the militia. Those who were arrested applied to North Carolina Supreme Court justice Richmond Pearson, and Pearson issued a writ of habeas corpus, freeing the offenders, and declaring that the militia in North Carolina had no legal power to seize people suspected of violating a Confederate law. The number of requests for writs multiplied, as did the number of deserters and those absent without leave from their regiments. Without regular Confederate soldiers in the vicinity to corral deserters, Jefferson Davis recommended that Governor Vance create a separate organization. In July, Vance authorized the Guard for Home Defense, better known as the home guard. All white males between the ages of eighteen and fifty, including those exempt from conscription, like militia officers, comprised the home guard.

Once again, Watauga County did not wait for official government action. "I am sorry to hear the tory has got to rebing the peopl thare agin," wrote Bennett Smith from Virginia in May 1863. "I was in hops they woold behave themselvs this Spring & Summer[.]" More importantly, Smith wrote, "I am in hops Bingham will keep them Strait I want him two ketch the last won of them & cend them to some fort where they will hav some thing to do

Harvey Bingham served as a lieutenant in the Thirty-seventh North Carolina troops and as a major in the Eleventh Battalion North Carolina Home Guard. *From Arthur's* History of Watauga County.

besids steel." The Bingham to whom Smith referred was Harvey Bingham, a former lieutenant in the Thirty-seventh Regiment who had resigned from the army in October 1862 by reason of "disease of the lungs." It appears that Bingham was already organizing a company some two months prior to the official creation of the home guard. He apparently was not the only one, as George Evans of Valle Crucis had written the governor, offering a company of seventy-five men over the age of forty. Whatever became of Evans's company is unknown. Bingham became captain of the Eleventh Battalion, North Carolina Home Guard not long thereafter. At some point, Bingham also established a camp on the upper part of Cove Creek, near the property (or possibly on the property) of A.J. McBride.[35]

The home guard was sorely needed in Watauga County. On August 3, 1863, a group of dissidents raided the Bethel community of Watauga County. They attacked the farm of George Evans, holding Evans's wife hostage while they ransacked the home and took "four or five hundred dollars worth" of property, not only belonging to Evans but also to the recently deceased William Skiles, the missionary at the Valle Crucis Episcopal Church. Then they proceeded to the home of Paul Farthing, surrounding it and demanding that he surrender. When Farthing refused to come out, the mob started firing into the home. The ladies of the home repaired upstairs and starting blowing horns, a predetermined signal that alerted their neighbors that help was needed. Upon hearing the warning, Thomas Farthing, Paul's older brother, grabbed his rifle and headed toward his brother's home. According to a friend, Thomas Farthing "unfortunately was discovered & fired upon by a guard stationed on the road side—two balls passing through his heart." After Farthing was killed, the attackers fled from the area. "The band was headed by a man by the name of Guy… They go in bands of 12 or 14—Nine of Paul Farthing's family were hurt & they found a good deal of blood about the porch & corner of the house." Blamed for the raid were the Guy brothers: Enoch, Canada and David. Enoch was around nineteen years of age. David was only seventeen. They appear on the Johnson County, Tennessee census in 1860. It appears that at least two of the brothers were later caught and executed for the crime. At some point, the father of the Guy brothers, Levi, was caught and hanged. It is interesting to note the two different accounts of his hanging. John Preston Arthur wrote in 1915, "Some time later Levi Guy was captured by some of the Confederate Home Guard and hanged, although he protested that he had done nothing more than shelter his own sons when they came to his house for foods and beds." In an article on his grandson, David Franklin Guy, we find: "Mr. Guy's grandfather, Levi Guy, who had served during the Mexican War, was such an ardent Union supporter and so outspoken in his beliefs, that he incurred the enmity of those who had Southern sentiments and was eventually taken out and hung."[36]

A little over a month later, more than thirty deserters, from either the Fifty-fourth or Sixty-third Virginia Regiment, were caught on their way from the Army of Tennessee back to Virginia. The group was masquerading as members of "Williams' Virginia Cavalry" in the process of joining their command. Two days after they left Asheville, the alarm was raised, and Major John Woodfin set out with twenty-five men. He overtook the band of deserters on the banks of the Watauga River, capturing thirty-six. The Virginia soldiers were sent to Camp Vance, and Woodfin returned a hero for having "returned 36 soldiers to duty and rid the country of a dangerous band of *free dealers* in horse flesh."[37]

Bennett Smith, in an earlier letter, chronicled a common soldier's thoughts about the desertion problem. Smith wanted a furlough to visit home but did

In 1863, Thomas Farthing was killed by bushwhackers, leaving behind his wife, Ermine, and son, Calvin. *Courtesy Cliff Farthing.*

not "sea any chance no way that is one of the last things they giv a man hear," he wrote to his wife. He then told of how there were "six runaway out of Hortons oald company a few nites ago & I thin there is several more a fixing to runaway the first oppertunity[.]" Smith himself had contemplated taking leave of the Thirty-seventh Regiment but wrote, "I dont think that I will go yet I want to wait fore the biggest crowd & then I will go." Smith, had he left, might have survived the war. He was dead six weeks after penning the above lines, dying in a hospital in Lynchburg, Virginia, on June 30, of "hydroxthrus" and/or "dropsy."[38]

Sometimes, social pressure was brought to bear upon those who left the army without permission. Empsey Gragg was thirty-two years old when he enlisted in the Fifty-eighth Regiment on July 7, 1862. On May 26 of the next year, he slipped off and came back to Watauga County. The members of Cove Creek Baptist Church learned that "Brother Emsey Gragg had left his Regiment in the Army without leave, [and] agreed to send a committee to see Brother Gragg and report the facts at the next meeting." At the next meeting, the committee reported that Gragg's wife had sent him a letter, "stating that she and his family were suffering for the want of something to live on and he had come home to see what he could do." Gragg himself was at the October meeting of his church and "made acknowledgement for his act of desertion and promised to return to his Regiment as soon as he could[.]" The members of the church agreed to not take action against him. Gragg reappears in the records of the Fifty-eighth Regiment in January–February 1864, listed as present but under arrest. He was reported as sick in May 1864 and then going over to the enemy, taking the Oath of Allegiance on June 14, 1864. There is a good chance he agreed to remain north of the Ohio River as a condition of his release.[39]

At other times, the truant men were simply caught and imprisoned, waiting for an escort, usually to Camp Vance in Morganton, where they could be loaded on a train and transported back to their regiments. In June 1863, Watauga County's Ransom Hayes was paid for keeping eight deserters from the Fifty-eighth in the local jail. Hayes received seventy-five cents per day for keeping Eli Harmon, Ransom Teaster, Elisha Trivett and Duke and Michael Ward, all members of Company D. Captain Bingham was advised that same month that the "Bush Whackers from Tenn" that he had apparently captured should be forwarded to Camp Holmes.[40]

On several occasions, both President Davis and Governor Vance issued proclamations pardoning men who were either absent without leave or deserters, providing that they returned to their regiments within a certain period of time. "There was an order sent round to all the companies in this regiment yesterday," wrote Nathan Horton (Thirty-seventh Regiment) on February 20, 1863. According to Horton, "All persons absent from their companies without leave must report to their respective companies by the 10th of March next and that those that fail to report by that time will be court martialed and shot as deserters, but those that come in by the 10th of March will not be punished at all." The difficulty with such sweeping acts of amnesty was that they caused more soldiers to desert, knowing that their unauthorized absences would be forgiven.[41]

Between August 1862 and August 1863, there seems to be just one man from Watauga County crossing over the mountains to join the Union army. George Dotson (Fifty-eighth Regiment) was a deserter who was caught in the Shady Valley area of Tennessee. According to the family, he was attempting to evade conscription officers when he was captured on March 24, 1863, and executed. Once the home guard was created, and assuming they began to search for deserters and those trying to avoid conscription, more men began to appear on the rolls of Federal regiments. Between August and November 1863, eighteen Watauga County citizens crossed over the mountains to the west and enlisted in the Thirteenth Tennessee Cavalry (U.S.). Of these eighteen men, thirteen were Confederate deserters. One came from the Beaver Dam district, one from the Valle Crucis district, six from the Cove Creek district, four from the Blue Ridge district and five from the Laurel Creek district. As can be seen from this, the men crossing over the lines to enlist in the Federal army were not just from one geographical spot in Watauga County. Comparing that list with the census, six could be considered in the poorest class, while ten came from middle-class families. Two men, William Story and Isaac Reece, were in their early forties; four others—John Potter, Jacob Younce, Barnett Yelton and Wiley Hatley—were in their late teens. Everyone else was in his twenties. Like the Banners in 1862, several were linked via kinship groups. John, Riley and Wiley Hately were all brothers. Likewise, William and Noah Story, brothers, enlisted with their first cousin Jesse Story.[42]

Some of the most costly and climactic battles of the war were waged in 1863, and the Tar Heel soldiers from Watauga County could often be found leading the way. The battle of Chancellorsville, Virginia, was fought in May 1863. The Thirty-seventh North Carolina Troops was in the woods that dark night when Stonewall Jackson's party rode through the lines. It was the Thirty-seventh that fired first, driving Jackson to the other side of the Orange Plank Road and into the guns of the Eighteenth North Carolina. The Eighteenth, thinking Jackson and his staff were Federal cavalry, opened fire, mortally wounding the Southern hero. The following day, the Thirty-seventh Regiment led the charge, and the two companies from Watauga lost six men killed. At Gettysburg, two months later, the regiment attacked Federal lines late in the day on July 1 and was involved in the climactic Pickett-Pettigrew-Trimble charge on July 3. Three additional Watauga County soldiers died as a result of the battle. Disease continued to be a worse foe than the Federal army: in 1863, fifteen Watauga County men in the Thirty-seventh Regiment perished from illness. The single Watauga County company in the First Cavalry lost three men killed in action through 1863. Disease ran rampant through the Fifty-eighth Regiment serving in the Army of Tennessee. Thirty-one Watauga County citizens perished in 1863. An additional three Watauga County men were killed at the battle of Chickamauga, Georgia, in September 1863.

Hardships of war, whether through the loss of a loved one in some distant place or hungry families at home, were all too real for Watauga County citizens as 1863 drew to a close. Yet the horrors of war were soon to hit even closer to home.

Chapter 4

1864

In September 1863, Confederate corps commander James Longstreet was ordered to take two divisions from the Army of Northern Virginia and join the Army of Tennessee. His troops were able to help win a Confederate victory at Chickamauga that month. Just prior to the battle of Chickamauga, Confederates evacuated east Tennessee. Later that year, Longstreet was ordered to re-take the city of Knoxville, which he attempted but failed to do. His troops spent the winter of 1863–64 encamped in east Tennessee. In the spring of 1864, Longstreet was ordered to rejoin the army in Northern Virginia, and the border of western North Carolina was left open to raids by both regular Federal soldiers and "Tories."

At some point in 1864, the home guard company in Watauga County was split into two companies. Harvey Bingham was promoted to major. Commanding Company A was George McGuire, who appears to have had no prior military experience. Commanding Company B was Jordan Cook, a former captain in the Thirty-seventh Regiment. The other officers in Company A were First Lieutenant Andrew J. McBride and Second Lieutenant A.P. Wilson. In Company B, the second lieutenant was William L. Bryant. Joseph Matherson was adjutant. Records for the home guard are sparse. There appear to have been around 154 officers and enlisted men in the two companies. Of these men, 33 had served in the army prior to joining the home guard. A few younger men, mere boys, possibly served in the home guard prior to joining the regular army. Of the members, 42 were above the age of forty, while 30 men were under twenty. Of the men identifiable in the

Little remains of the home guard base known as Camp Mast, now marked by this North Carolina Civil War Trail Marker erected in 2012. *Author's collection.*

census, 6 were upper class, including John "Jack" Horton, Lewis Farthing and Henry Taylor. Those 3 alone owned a combined nineteen slaves. There were 64 members of the middle class and just 29 of the poorer class. Those on the lower end include Jonathan Anderson, a free person of color.

Often, one of the companies of the home guard was on duty while the other company was at home, taking care of their farms. Enoch Swift, a member of McGuire's company, recalled later in life that the camp moved from the McBride property, farther down Cove Creek, to the property of Lorenzo Whittington, across the road from the old Cove Creek School. One Federal soldier, captured while attempting to pass through the mountains to the Union lines in east Tennessee, was taken to Camp Mast and described the camp as having "but one street and a row of cabins on either side. There were but fifteen cabins in all, twelve of which were for the privates, one for the officers, and two for horses." According to oral history, the camp was located in a hollow, an attempt to protect the soldiers when the winter winds howled.[43]

Bingham's home guard had an unenviable assignment. Hunting deserters and conscript dodgers meant pursuing people's fathers, brothers, husbands and sons and returning them to the army. Often, the people that the home guard members were hunting were their own extended family and friends.

On April 7, 1864, Governor Vance wrote to Confederate Secretary of War James Seddon, "In the counties of Mitchell, Yancey and Watauga the tories and deserters are in strong force." There are many tales of the depredations committed by "tories" and rogues. According to one postwar account, bushwhackers

> *came one night to the* [Alexander] *Wilson home* [in the Beaver Dam community], *ransacked the house of every bite of food and of all the portable chattels they could find and then proceeded to the Hagaman house, where they did the same thing and drove off the horses. They even went through the rooms, and, unable to carry off the bedclothes, they burned them in the fireplace through sheer love of vandalism, and left the Hagamans to sleep without covering.*
>
> [Hugh Hagaman] *followed the bushwhackers and overtook them where they had camped in a hollow. The stolen horses had been picketed some distance from the camp and had been left unguarded. Hugh quietly untied his horses and started home with them.*
>
> *Before he reached home it was dark: hence, he put up at a neighbor's house for the night. The bushwhackers, missing the horses, gave chase and overtook Hugh at the neighbor's house, called out to him, and demanded the horses. For answer, Hugh cocked his gun and said "You can kill me, but I'll get the first one who approaches this door. Come on! Who wants to be first?"*
>
> *There was some mumbling among the bushwhackers, but as none wanted the honor of being first, the entire band turned and galloped away and left Hugh to pursue his way homeward with his horses.*[44]

Some of the depredations were likewise committed by the home guard. According to a typescript manuscript about the Civil War in Watauga County, there was a cemetery in the Deep Gap area that bore a tombstone for a man named "Black" who was killed by the home guard. In the Aho community, a man named Hines was shot by the home guard as he begged for money. Supposedly, Bettie and Lucy Story saw that the man got a decent burial. And in the Dutch Creek community, a man by the name of Shoemaker was killed by the home guard and buried in Valle Crucis. Dugger records that Shoemaker's father came and removed the remains to Alexander County. Yet a different source tells that Nathan Harrison left to join the Union army, and a member of the home guard went to Richlands in Caldwell County and "shot a Nelson man but found out he was mistaken and had shot the wrong man." Harrsion's family evidently never knew his fate as a victim of mistaken identity. Chances are we will never definitely know the validity of these stories.[45]

Toward the end of April 1864, the adjutant general was forced to write to Bingham about reports that his command had been seizing the property of disloyal citizens. Vance ordered that the property be restored "to its rightful owners…which may have been seized. The fact of a man's disloyalty does not warrant confiscation of his estate and the Governor desires that no North Carolina company shall be guilty of plundering or attempting to confiscate property." The previous year, the adjutant general had written to Bingham, "Your men are under the articles of War, and if guilty of mutiny can be court marshalled and shot." John Jones, a confirmed Unionist, complained after the war that James Wilborn Trivette, a member of the home guard, had threatened Jones with arrest, death, the death of his wife and also "took my gun [and] robed my house of bed clothing wearing clothes provisions crockery weare [and] other things." As illustrated with the letters coming from the adjutant general, not everything was well within the home guard. The adjutant general had written to Captain Jordan Cook, advising him, "When your men refuse to obey your orders they are subject to the rules and articles of war & when you order them out for orders from the office." The adjutant general advised Cook to send out detachments of men to bring in his wayward home guard members to drills or on expeditions to round up deserters. These statements combined might lead to the idea that Watauga County's Home Guard Battalion was not particularly rigorous in its discipline. In the defense of home guard members, their job was extremely difficult.[46]

There were some who sought ingenious ways to avoid service. Landon Snider left Ashe County and went to his sister's home in the Beaver Dam community. He was caught and taken to Camp Mast and turned over to the authorities, who placed a guard over him. Snider was determined to escape and, late one evening, "made a break for it and ran in the direction of the place where the horses were haltered. Shots rang out," and one of the members of the home guard "ran in the direction of the place where the horses were tied and observed something lying on the ground. And struggling violently he stooped down and said, 'Oh, yes, Mr. Snider, I told you we would shoot!' Just then a terrible blow landed" on the head of the home guard member. Instead of Snider being wounded, it was one of the horses, and Snider was soon on his way elsewhere.[47]

Goulder Carroll Harmon, pictured with his wife, Lucinda Ward Harmon, served in the Fifty-eighth North Carolina Troops but was dropped for unknown reasons in 1864. *Courtesy Terry Harmon.*

Yet another case is that of John Walker from the Valle Crucis community. Walker was a member of the home guard but no longer had a desire to serve. He also had no desire to abscond, which would have meant forfeiting his social standing in the community and being forced to live in the brush. Walker formulated a plan in which he was captured by six women and two men, all dressed as Federal soldiers. One evening, the "Federal soldiers" marched into Walker's front yard, stopping at the front door and rapping for admittance. John and his women folk, with white faces, appeared and opened the door. The soldiers demanded Walker's surrender. "There was a parley, John's women pleading for him, with tear-bedimmed eyes." The soldiers had to tear Walker "away from the arms of his family." Word soon spread that there were Yankees in the area, and "France and Wilts Beech...were started on horses" to alert the Home Guard. Walker was "taken to a ridge and rock cliff just above" a mill and was "fed by Elisha [Coffey] whenever he went out to feed his hogs. It was about one week later that John walked into his home, apparently much crippled up and sorely distraught, but bearing an iron-clad paper-writing with his signature attached, a duplicate of the one he declared the Yankees in Tennessee had compelled him to sign while in captivity." Walker's ruse worked, and he was not required to perform duty with the home guard, at least not at that time.[48]

While there were some people who chose to leave the county during the war, like militia captain Hugh Nelson, others thought that Watauga County held some degree of safety. Dr. James G. Rivers left Carter County, Tennessee, and came to Watauga County during the war. He served as a surgeon for the Eleventh Battalion North Carolina home guard in 1864.[49]

In June 1864, Captain George W. Kirk, a Unionist from east Tennessee, led a raid into Burke County. Kirk and his small band of Union soldiers attacked Camp Vance near Morganton, destroying the camp, releasing prisoners and capturing many of the recently mustered but unarmed junior reserves. As Kirk retreated back up the mountain, he was forced to fight several small skirmishes. In one of these skirmishes, he actually used some of his prisoners as human shields and laughed when they were struck and killed. Once back in present-day Avery County, he allowed the home of Colonel Palmer to be burned and then proceeded to destroy the Cranberry Iron Works. The mines provided small amounts of iron ore to the Confederacy during much of the war. Approximately forty men were detailed to work at the mines, and these men were exempt from conscription. While the names of most of these men are not known, it is recorded that both George W. Dugger and Napoleon Banner worked at the mines. Kirk's daring raid was praised by his superiors and showed many that the interior of western North Carolina lay open to attack.[50]

When Kirk led his raid in June 1864, he was a captain in the Second North Carolina Mounted Infantry (U.S.), a regiment largely made up of dissidents, Unionists and Confederate deserters. Kirk had recently received permission to recruit his own regiment, which in time would become known as the Third North Carolina Mounted Infantry (U.S.). In the winter of 1865, Kirk was promoted to colonel of this regiment. These two organizations seldom functioned as regiments. Often, the men moved about in small bands through the countryside, their plundering and rapine knowing no boundaries.

A slow trickle of men continued crossing over the mountains to join the Union army in 1864. Melmoth Bowles, Waitsel Hodges and Marion Wilson joined those from Watauga County already serving in the Thirteenth Tennessee Cavalry (U.S.). Lieutenant Andrew W. Fondren, a Carter County native in the Thirteenth, recalled recruiting in Watauga County. Thirteen others joined Kirk's new regiment. However, there was not a mass exodus of

George W. Kirk (right) pictured with his father, Alexander Kirk, (standing) and brother John Kirk (left) was promoted to colonel of the Third North Carolina Mounted Infantry (U.S.) and led a rapacious band of "scoundrels of thieves" that became a scourge upon Watauga County. *Courtesy Matt Bumgarner.*

men crossing over from Watauga. James Hartley and Lindsey Rash crossed over in June; Jesse Keller in July; Moses Triplett and Thomas Barlow the first of August, with James and John Ervin following later that month; and Peter Danner, John Gragg, Calvin Tucker and Darby Triplett in November.[51]

For some unknown reason, five Watauga County citizens chose to join the Third Tennessee Mounted Infantry (U.S.) in August 1864. They all listed their places of enlistment as Boone, so it is possible that there was a recruiter for this regiment in the area that month. The Third Tennessee (U.S.) was a one-hundred-day regiment, possibly organized to provide defensive troops as front-line regiments moved elsewhere. Its members were all mustered out in November 1864. The five recruits were Enoch Fletcher, Elias Isaacs, Noah Isaacs, Thomas Bingham and Spencer Fletcher. Thomas Bingham was a younger brother of home guard commander Harvey Bingham.

Although information is once again sparse, there was a type of underground railroad that ran through Watauga County. But instead of being a pathway to freedom for slaves, it was a conduit for dissidents and escaped Federal prisoners out of the Federal prison at Salisbury, North Carolina. John "Jack" Horton of Boone recalled helping two sets of escaped prisoners. Horton not only hid them but also fed them and allowed them to use his horses for part of the way to the Union lines. According to Dugger, once these escapees reached Blowing Rock, they were met "by one of three scouts, Keith Blalock, Harrison Church or Jim Hartley, and conducted by Shulls Mills, Dutch Creek and Hanging Rock Gap to Banner Elk, where after getting some relief from fatigue and hunger, they went on by Cranberry to…Shell Creek, Tennessee, where they were taken in charge by Dan Ellis." Dugger went on to recount how on one occasion, a man came from a nearby thicket to his home and asked Dugger's mother to fix food for six men. Dugger's mother told the man to go and wait, and the children would bring the food. "We were met at the edge of the woods," wrote Dugger, "and conducted to where the remaining five were seated on logs. I knew the guide…to be Harrison Church." Dugger learned that the party had encountered the home guard; one of the small group, Major Ducheney (probably Lieutenant Lawrence Ducheney, First Massachusetts Cavalry), had "a Minnie-ball hitting his knife in his pocket, had drove it against the flesh with such force that he was limping."[52]

The Banners, of present-day Banner Elk, were just one family who could be trusted to help those evading capture. Lewis Banner, whose sons were serving in the Union army, was usually willing to provide escaped Federal soldiers with food and, at times, a guide. The escapees hid in an area known as the Land of Goshen. On the eastern side of Watauga County, the Story family likewise helped those seeking to make their way across the mountains. One early historian recalled that the "homes of the Storys were open to the Federal soldiers and sympathizers, and the women of the families often waded the streams to carry food to outliers, Bettie and Lucie once taking a wounded Yankee to Coffey's Gap in the night on an old horse." There were undoubtedly others who were friendly or other spots deemed safe. The Blalocks and their "gang" supposedly hid out on Myria Knob, off the turnpike running between Valle Crucis and Blowing Rock.[53]

Francis Hosmer, of the Fourth Vermont Infantry, was captured at the battle of Reams Station, Virginia, on June 23, 1864. While on a train heading south out of Lynchburg, Hosmer and another soldier, Corporal H.T. Gorham, jumped off the train and started heading west through Wilkes County and into Watauga. The pair ran into a larger group, which Hosmer estimated at a little over 132 men, about half Confederate deserters and the other half dissidents. Their guide, learning that the party had been spotted by two women out picking blackberries, abandoned the group and continued unencumbered to east Tennessee. The party was soon discovered by "Uncle Billy Cook," a "man of sandy complexion, full beard, about five feet five inches high, probably fifty-five years of age, of pronounced theological views, and a Union man, who had proclaimed his loyalty from the first, and declared that if the Confederacy compelled him to fight he proposed to commence on his own premises. So far he had been watched, but not molested." Food was soon delivered, and the group moved to a laurel thicket in the Story settlement. Food was brought by others, but feeding such a large group was a burden. Since the mountains were full of local troops looking for this group, Cook advised them to split up "into small parties and make your way the best you can. Some of you can get through in that way, and some will likely be caught." Hosmer and Gorham eventually ran into the home guard and were re-captured. They were imprisoned in "an old building," possibly at Camp Mast, with Uncle Billy Cook. But the group denied that they had ever met Cook before and probably saved his life. "The next day under a strong guard," recorded Hosmer, "we were marched over the mountain to the little hamlet of Boone, and there quartered in the county jail, an old log building, of two stories, and four rooms." Confined upstairs were the Story sisters, who so often had helped Union soldiers. Hosmer believed that they were apprehended about the same time as Cook. Hosmer and Gorham were taken the next day to Camp Vance and then to Salisbury.[54]

One pair to make it through more successfully were Junius Browne and Albert Richardson, newspaper reporters captured in 1863 after their ship was struck by Confederate artillery fire and sunk in the Mississippi River. The two were taken to Richmond and then Salisbury before escaping and making their way west through Wilkes County. They arrived in Watauga County on January 1, 1864, and were taken in by a Unionist and permitted to sleep on a featherbed with several coverlets in the upper part of a storehouse. In Browne's account, written just a year after the close of the war, he confessed that he could not sleep: "The infernal vermin [body lice], of which we had not gotten rid, torturing us exceedingly." They found a guide to take them through the county and, due to the weather, found the roads almost clear of guards. At one point, they were forced to hide behind some logs, avoiding mounted men. However, the "weather [was] cold and [the] wind cutting," and they seemed to be always wet, falling "into a number of mountain streams" on their journey.[55]

Clashes between Bingham's home guard, along with loyal Confederate citizens, and the deserters, outliers, escaped prisoners and Unionists from

Tennessee were numerous. The *Raleigh Conservative*, in a story possibly connected to the above account, wrote in August 1864, "Capt. McMillan with his cavalry and the Watauga Home Guards, captured, a few days ago in Watauga County, forty-one and killed five of the Yadkin Tories and deserters, as they were making their way to Tennessee, in order to obtain reinforcements with a view of returning to the Western counties and controlling the election in favor of Mr. Holden." Holden was Raleigh newspaperman William W. Holden, who chose to run against Governor Zebulon Vance in 1864. A year earlier, Holden had joined ideologically with Northern Democrats, encouraging people to rise up and demand the war to cease. His words spread like fire through the state, and in the summer of 1863, over one hundred peace meetings were held. Such a meeting was held in the Stony Fork section on August 15, 1863. John R. Hodges was called upon to chair the meeting, with A.W. Penley, secretary. The resolutions approved that day probably held true for the majority of people in the counties, tired of the war.

> *Resolved, That peace cannot be restored merely by fighting. This we think is now apparent to all.*
>
> *Resolved, That the present bloody and inhuman war has raged long enough, without any profit or material advantage to either the North or South; we therefore call upon our next Congress to use their utmost endeavors to obtain a cessation of hostilities, or a termination of our present struggles in a just, honorable, and lasting peace.*
>
> *Resolved, That Western North Carolina has furnished over her quota of men and means, and has no slaves to work her soil; we think it expedient that no further call should be made on her for troops…*
>
> *Resolved, That W.W. Holden is one the ablest and boldest defenders of the rights of the people in the State, and we recommend the Standard to every lover of liberty, and to all who are opposed to despotism at home or abroad. We also endorse the course pursued by his Excellency, Gov. Vance.*[56]

The peace movement split the conservative party in North Carolina, with Vance leading the War Wing and Holden leading the Peace Wing. Troops were ordered into the mountain counties to protect polling places. While it appears that no outside troops were in Watauga County, portions of the Sixty-eighth Regiment were in Wilkes and Mitchell Counties. Vance won a sweeping statewide victory in August 1864. While 95 people voted for Holden in Watauga County, 272 voted for Vance.[57]

Vance's reelection did nothing to curtail the violence. Much of the hostility seemed to be centered around livestock. An account from the Sampson Gap area told how a local Confederate agent by the name of Todd impressed the horse of Betsy Story Nelson. As Todd rode off whistling "Dixie," Nelson yelled at him that Todd would be "whistling 'Dixie' in hell before the next day was over." Nelson supposedly recruited some men from the community, and the next day, Todd's body was found floating in Joe's Fork Creek, with the horse "tied up at Betsy Nelson's gate." In another narrative, Sarah Adams Wilson, whose husband was away fighting in the army, personally went to east Tennessee to recover her horse. Despite being threatened by the horse thieves, she returned not only with the horse but also with blankets that her mother had made. Wilson tied the horse up near the house and "sat all night waiting in the open door with a gun across her lap." The thieves failed to appear. In September 1864, A.C. Allen, who was managing a farm in the Meat Camp area for Hamilton Brown of Wilkes County, wrote the following letter to his employer: "I aimed to come down last week but Wm. had to be gone fighting Torys and I had to watch as well as Prey. All things is getting along very well...We captured Granville Smoot and Brooks...Smoot and Brooks will not trouble you any more they went up the spout...I am compeld to use all Exertions to keep our property safe." Smoot and Brooks piloted Union men from or through Wilkes County, through Elk Cross Roads and into Ashe County and Tennessee. According to Arthur, they "were killed on the left of the road leading to Blowing Rock...by the home guard." Some tried less violent ways to retrieve their property. Alfred Thomas ran an advertisement in an Abington, Virginia newspaper, stating that he was willing to pay $200 for the return of his stolen horse.[58]

In the fall of 1864, a group of nine robbed and shot James Farthing. Proceeding on to the home of Reuben Farthing, they stole some horses before retreating. Word was sent to Bingham, who arrived with eighteen men. After cooking three days' worth of rations, Bingham set out and recovered the horses near Balm. At the same time, Bingham moved into the Poga community, capturing Jim Clawson and driving "off some beef cattle." In the Heaton area, they captured Bill Gwyn, a Federal soldier who had deserted the Eighth Tennessee Cavalry (U.S.) a year earlier. They then met Linda Smith, "riding a mare followed by a mule colt and carrying her part of some leather...In a vain effort to save her mare and leather she pleaded her children's bare feet and her unploughed fields, but in retaliation for a raid that took the blankets from the children's beds on Beaver Dam they considered it fair."

Bingham then captured shoemaker Bill Shull and camped that night in Balm. James Hartley, the Union guide, was notified and, taking thirteen or eighteen men, lay in ambush at Bower's Gap. Bingham decided to return via a different route, and Polly Aldridge passed through Bingham's column, asking each man, "Did you men see my spotted cow down here anywhere?" She quickly found Hartley and informed him that Bingham had "started up an old road that led across the east end of Beech Mountain to Watauga River at the mouth of Cove Creek." Hartley then redeployed his men and, a mile above the Balm community, engaged Bingham's men. According to Dugger, the "first volley killed the...mare and mortally wounded Dick Kilby." Hartley moved Kilby to the shade of an oak tree, his group charged, "and a battle raged all over the timbered knob." Hartley, who is thought to have carried a Spencer repeating rifle, shot Elliott Bingham, Major Bingham's youngest brother, as Elliott stepped out from behind, taking aim at Hartley. "Jack, I'm killed, and they'll get you," Elliott reportedly told A.J. McBride, who was nearby. "Leave me, and save yourself." Dugger wrote that James Hartley saw his brother with Bingham's men and yelled, "Ha Cal! Come here and shake hands with your brother," a request that "Cal" answered "with a shot that cut [James's] coat." Bingham ordered his men to retreat, an action that caused McBride, wielding a shotgun, to curse and swear. Elliott Bingham was taken to John Banner's house, "where his mother got to him that evening and [Dugger] saw her sad face as she administered to the parched lips of her darling boy who died the next day." The "Battle of Beech Mountain" even made statewide news. One Raleigh newspaper reported, "There was quite a severe fight...in Watauga county between a party of deserters, under one Jim Hartley, and a detachment of Home Guards, under Maj. Bingham. Four of the Home Guard wounded, one mortally. Eight deserters reported killed and several wounded." Later historians recorded that none of Hartley's group was actually wounded or killed.[59]

Major Bingham was later awarded a resolution of thanks by the General Assembly of North Carolina for his zealous attention to capturing deserters and bushwhackers not only in Watauga County but in surrounding counties as well.[60]

If the constant threat of deserters, Unionists and the home guard was not enough, bands of rogue Confederate cavalry showed up at least twice in 1864. In April, a Confederate officer wrote to Vance that he had encountered elements of Brigadier General John C. Vaughn's cavalry brigade as the officer rode into Watauga County. A half-mile after passing Vaughn,

> *I met some half doz. of his soldiers, and I continued to meet them in squads of from two to twenty, all the way to this place* [Boone]—*straggling along without the shadow of organization or discipline. In this manner they continued to come through for ten days. The whole command (some seventeen or eighteen hundred men) just disbanded, and turned loose to pillage the inhabitants, and thoroughly did they perform their work. It was not merely stealing but open and above board highway robbery. They would enter houses violently breaking open every door, and helping themselves to what suited their various fancies—not provisions only, but everything, from horses down to ladies breast pins.*[61]

Vaughn's cavalry apparently returned toward the end of the year. On December 6, 1864, Vaughn wrote to Vance that the citizens of Watauga County had hanged two of his soldiers. "No one can more deplore the *quasi* warfare between the troops and the citizens than myself," Vance answered Vaughn's missive. "But sir, the conduct of your men…in parts of our mountain country has been sufficient to drive our people to desperation. The stories of robbery and outrage by them would fill a volume and would fully justify the immediate indiscriminate slaughter of all men caught with the proofs of their villainy. From looking upon them as their gallant protectors, thousands in their bitterness of hearts have come to regard them as their deadliest enemies."[62]

War had come in earnest to those in Watauga County. Likewise, the war entered a new phase in the armies as well. In 1864, soldiers began fighting from elaborate trenches and field works, built to protect the troops. Soldiers quickly threw up works during the Overland Campaign in Virginia and the North Georgia Campaign. Troops from Watauga County were involved in battles like the Wilderness, Spotsylvania Court House, North Anna River and Cold Harbor in Virginia in the spring of 1864. In North Georgia, local troops fought at Rocky Face Ridge, Resaca and Kolb's Farm during the same period of time. Starting in late spring, the armies became bogged down in the trenches around Petersburg and to the east of Richmond, as well as those surrounding Atlanta. The Fifty-eighth Regiment and the rest of the Army of Tennessee abandoned Atlanta on September 2, 1864, and moved north into Alabama and Tennessee. However, the Fifty-eighth was left behind at Columbia, Tennessee, and thus escaped the disastrous battles of Franklin and Nashville. Those killed in battle or who died of disease were fewer than in previous years. Attrition had taken its toll. Only two Watauga County members of the Thirty-seventh Regiment were killed in battle, while eight died of disease. The First Cavalry lost two Watauga County men killed in battle and four to disease, while the Fifty-eighth Regiment lost two on the battlefield, two to disease and one to execution. Desertions picked up, and these men did not return.

People usually look forward to a new year: it brings hope and promise of better days. For those living along the Watauga River and Cove Creek, this new year, 1865, only promised more doom, despair and loss.

Chapter 5

1865

Over the course of three years, the Confederacy had slowly applied more and more pressure upon the populace. Conscription, originally requiring enlistment for men from ages eighteen to thirty-five, was extended to men ages seventeen to fifty. The youngest served in the junior reserve, while those over forty-five constituted the senior reserves. Either the law was never applied to Watauga County, or local boys and older men chose to ignore it, for no local residents appear to have joined either organization. In April 1863, the Confederate government passed the very unpopular tax-in-kind. Farmers were required to pay a portion of their harvest—wheat, oats, corn, rice, potatoes, fodder, sugar, cotton, wool, tobacco and rye—along with a 10 percent tax on slaughtered hogs. Agents were appointed to collect the taxes. The name of Watauga's agent and the amount he collected are unknown. The record for collection of state taxes in Watauga in 1864 is also missing, possibly because they were never collected or recorded.

Winter did not bring a respite from war to the people in Watauga County. In January 1865, James Carroll was out trying to recruit men for the Federal army. He recalled in 1886 that he and George W. Perkins were "at the house of William Triplett trying to recruit him; that while on their way from Triplett's house to the widow Carroll's…they came upon a party of rebels, being part of the Watauga Home Guard, commanded by Lieut. Lewis Bryant; that said rebels fired upon them, wounding [Carroll] in the right side and hip." One ball entered the right breast of Carroll, breaking one rib and damaging his lung before exiting out his back. The second ball struck Carroll in the thigh, "causing paralysis of the whole leg." John Elrod, a member of the home guard, recalls that several shots were fired at Perkins and Carroll. Perkins supposedly escaped, while Elrod carried Carroll to his mother's house, the widow Carroll referred to above, and dressed his wounds before leaving.[63]

There were some who carried on their own personal wars while the bigger conflict raged. In 1864, Keith Blalock and his band captured William Coffey in Caldwell County. William and his brother Reuben Coffey, step-uncles of Blalock, were "pronounced Southern men" and had zealously sought out men who legally should have been in the Confederate army. Blalock's discharge papers meant little to them, and when he started piloting men through the lines to the Union army, there was open hostility, not only with his step-uncles, but with other Confederate conscription officers. On one occasion, Keith and Malinda were chased up Grandfather Mountain and forced to hide in a hog pen. Keith was wounded in the melee, and he blamed Robert Green of Caldwell County for wounding him. Blalock eventually accosted Green on the road between Blowing Rock and the Globe, shooting and wounding Green. William Coffey was later caught out plowing his field. The Blalock band took him to James Gragg's mill, where a man named Perkins killed him. In 1864, the Blalock band attempted to capture Carroll Moore, but Keith had his eye shot out in the process and was forced to flee to east Tennessee to recover.[64]

Governor Vance allowed the creation of a battalion under the command of Major A.C. Avery in early 1865 to protect the mountain counties and assist the home guard. Avery's battalion was headquartered in Morganton and supplied with arms from Raleigh. A part of the battalion, Captain John Carson's company, from McDowell County, rode first to McCaleb Coffey's farm in Coffey's Gap. Not finding him there, they traveled on to Austin Coffey's home, where neighbor John Boyd recognized Austin and arrested him. Coffey was taken to an empty house "about half way between Shull's Mill and Blowing Rock." According to an 1870 letter written by Guthridge Garland, Coffey was tied up to a tree most of the night. "In the morning his ropes were loosened from the tree. He laid down by the fire and one of the braves shot his brains out. They took him off and hid him behind a log." Arthur relates that John Walker, possibly the same Walker who had previously staged his capture and parole, was ordered to kill Coffey but refused and that "Robert Glass, or Anders, volunteered…and while the old man slept shot him through the head." Coffey's body was then dumped in a laurel thicket. A week later, a dog was spotted "with a human hand in his mouth." A search was made, and his body was discovered and buried. The date of Austin Coffey's death is given as February 26, 1865.[65]

That same month, Avery's Battalion was ordered to supply the Eleventh Battalion Home Guard with long arms. While the battalion was en route, a raid on Camp Mast originated in the Banner Elk settlement. Company A, under Captain McGuire, was at the camp, while Company B, under Lieutenant William Bryant, was stationed in Boone. Major Bingham and Lieutenant Matherson were absent, possibly conferring with the home guard commander in Ashe County about a joint operation. A man by the name of James Champion gathered, according to Dugger, about 25 members of the Thirteenth Tennessee Cavalry (U.S.), along with 50 other men, armed "with muskets, shotguns and hog rifles," although Arthur adds that "many of them had no weapons at all" and reports varying numbers. They set out on the evening of February 4, proceeding to Valle Crucis, where they "killed one of Henry Taylor's beeves, cooked it and had supper." While finishing supper, Champion told the men of his plans and advised that anyone "who expected to loot or rob or burn or destroy any property not strictly contraband, he must fall out." Arthur states that 20 of the 123 men present by his count fell out and returned to their homes. Using James Isaacs as a guide, the band crossed Brushy Fork Creek at Vilas and arrived at the camp about dawn. The ground was frozen; they believed that "the clang of their horses' shoes had aroused every dog in Christendom, and just before reaching the camp a flock of sheep became frightened and fled helter-skelter down the ridge toward the camp." Yet the home guardsmen, possibly due to the weather, had failed to place a picket around their camp, an odd omission considering that McGuire had sent word to Bryant that he expected an attack on the camp.

Champion divided his force into three sections: one under Isaac Reece, one under Aaron Von Cannon and the third under his personal command. The men surrounded the camp, with every other man ordered to build a campfire. As the home guard soldiers struggled from their cabins, they were greeted by the ring of fires in the early morning light. General H. Franklin, "a fine looking Yankee soldier," and a lieutenant in the Thirteenth Tennessee Cavalry (U.S.), stood on the hillside with a white flag. He headed into the camp, possibly escorted by Henry Lineback, also of the Thirteenth Cavalry, with a note for McGuire, demanding the surrender of the camp. McGuire had half an hour to decide, or Champion would attack. After polling his men, McGuire informed Champion that sixty men had voted to surrender, while eleven voted to stay and fight. McGuire surrendered his men, and

Champion ordered his men to burn the camp. Soon thereafter, Champion had his men and the prisoners back on the road, moving toward the Banner Elk settlement. Dugger recalled that the men "marched in pairs—two guards with guns, behind two prisoners, each with his blanket rolled and tied in a circle that passed over one shoulder and under one arm." When Lieutenant Bryant arrived from Boone a little later, he discovered the men gone and the camp in smoking ruins. Many thought that McGuire was complicit to the surrender, as he was seen riding away with the Federal officers. While that is possible, he simply could have been afforded the privilege of an honorable retreat because he was an officer.

The prisoners were split into two groups for the night, and local people prepared rations. Some of the prisoners, like Silas and A.J. McBride, were able to steal away in the night. The remaining prisoners set out early the next morning, and upon reaching Shell Creek, just over the Tennessee line, those who had voted to surrender were paroled and released, allowed to return to their homes, while those who had voted to fight it out were escorted on to prison. Among those captured and sent to prison were local Confederate enrolling officer Lieutenant James H. Webb, Paul Farthing and his nephew Reuben Farthing, who were all sent to Camp Chase in Ohio. Webb was later paroled, but the Farthings both died of disease while incarcerated.[66]

Apparently Captain Cook wrote to Governor Vance, informing him of the surrender of McGuire's company and the loss of Camp Mast. Cook wanted regular Confederate troops sent to the area, but Vance had none to send. The adjutant general advised Cook to reorganize the home guard, "so that the whole arms bearing population may be put on duty for their own defence…you must be aware that the condition of things demand that every one should assist in the defence of his own home and no time should be lost in preparing for it." Likewise, the adjutant general wrote to Bingham, demanding both a report concerning the surrender of the camp and a report explaining Bingham's absence.[67]

Cook, on reading the adjutant general's missive, probably did not realize just how little time they did have. About six weeks later, word arrived that Federal soldiers were again on the move. Captain Cook assembled his home guard company in Boone, possibly in an attempt to reorganize his men. It was a common belief that the rumored approach was just "another little squad coming to fool us," just as Hartley had done in 1864, and Champion had done a few weeks earlier. The home guard was mistaken. This was not a little band of locally recruited men but regular, combat-hardened troops.[68]

In 1865, Major General George W. Stoneman led the only full-scale Union incursion into Watauga County. *Library of Congress.*

Federal major general George Stoneman was named commander of the District of East Tennessee in February 1865. Overall Federal commander U.S. Grant ordered Stoneman to lead a raid into South Carolina, but Stoneman failed to get his men underway prior to Sherman's capture of Columbia. Orders then came for Stoneman to move into western North Carolina, with ambitions to capture Salisbury and liberate the prisoners held there. This movement placed a sizable body of Federal cavalry in the rear of both principal Confederate armies in the field: Lee's army in Virginia and Johnston's army in eastern North Carolina.

Stoneman's Raid, as the action is generally called, was composed of six thousand cavalry and a few pieces of artillery. The raid started in late March 1865. On March 28, Stoneman sent a detachment of the Twelfth Kentucky Cavalry, under Major Myles Keogh, into Boone. It is possible that the first person with whom they came into contact was Jacob Councill. According to an account written not too many years after the war, Councill "was plowing with a negro. He was...a prudent, quiet man...He was shot down in cold blood, notwithstanding his piteous cries for mercy, because, upon the negro's statement, he was 'an infernal rebel.'" Another account states that Councill was in the act of putting away his harness when he came to the door and was shot and killed. While there is nothing to confirm Councill's being an "infernal rebel," he was a thirty-five-year-old father of at least three children, not a slave owner, and a member of the home guard.[69]

Seeing the blue-coated cavalrymen ride into Boone from the west, some home guardsmen fled, while others went into the house of James W. Councill, where they opened fire on the Kentucky soldiers. Opening fire themselves, the cavalrymen charged into the town. Hearing the commotion, Mary Councill, holding one of her children, stepped out on the front porch of her home. She was greeted by "a volley of balls[that] splintered the woodwork all around her" but escaped back inside unhurt. The rest of the home guard scattered, with the Federal cavalry in hot pursuit. John Bryan was "struck by a soldier...with a gun." John Brown's ankle was broken, while Thomas Holder was wounded in the hip and groin. A.J. McBride, who had escaped after being captured at Camp Mast, was shot in the breast, "the ball followed a rib and lodged near his spine." Calvin Green had attempted to surrender but was fired upon. So he retrieved his rifle "and fought, loading and firing till he was shot down and left for dead...[shattering] the arm of one of the Federal soldiers." Warren Green "was killed while holding up his hands in token of surrender." Also killed was Ephraim Norris, who was just shy of his forty-sixth birthday. Others, like fifteen-year-old Steel Frazier, continued to fight on, although the account of his killing at least one of his pursuers is possibly exaggerated.[70]

The "battle of Boone" was actually just a mere skirmish, lasting but a few moments. Federals swarmed the town, and Stoneman's men arrested just about every male in the vicinity. The number of captured was reported as sixty-eight. Among those arrested was John "Jack" Horton. Once it was proved that Horton was a "Union man," he was released. Horton then informed Stoneman that two men being held in the jail in Boone were also Union men. Their names were "Wilburne, another Joseph Harrison."[71]

Federal surgeons established a makeshift field hospital in the home of Jacob Councill. McBride was forced to lie on his stomach on the floor while a doctor cut the bullet out of his back. It was rumored that one of the Federals wounded by Calvin Miller had his arm amputated that evening. Stoneman spent the evening at the home of John Councill, which was given special protection against depredations. Federal soldiers continued to move through Watauga County for at least a day after Stoneman left. Brigadier General Alvan Gillem ordered the jail, along with the majority of court records, burned. Those captured were placed under guard and sent on into Tennessee. Lewis Farthing was among the captured. Seeing a chance to escape while on the march, Farthing raced into a "clump of laurel," throwing his blanket over a bush as he went. This was followed by the crack of rifles, which filled Farthing's blanket with holes.[72]

Orders went out that the Federal column was to be split, with a portion heading through Deep Gap toward Wilkesboro, while the other group made its way through Blowing Rock and into Caldwell County. Washington Shearer, a slave belonging to Robert Shearer, recalled after the war that he was abducted by some Federal cavalrymen and forced to go to Wilkesboro. Once there, he was released but became a "waiting man" for Captain Munday of the Fifteenth Pennsylvania Cavalry. It is unclear if this was a voluntary act, or if Washington Shearer was forced to do so. Regardless, Shearer went all the way to Huntsville, Alabama, with the Fifteenth. Shearer recalled seeing another slave from Watauga County, Wash Horton, in Wilkesboro, riding a stolen horse belonging to William Vandyke. Stoneman's command was eventually reunited and ventured into Virginia, before returning on April 9 to North Carolina. The Federals worked their way through Mocksville and Mooresville, fighting a pitched battle, which they won, at Salisbury on April 12. This was followed by a defeat when the Federals attempted to take the bridge over the Yadkin River. Stoneman then proceeded to work his way back west, destroying Confederate supply depots in Salisbury and Statesville in the process. Stoneman's men moved through Taylorsville and Lenoir, but the grand plan to liberate the Salisbury prisoners never materialized. Most of the prisoners had already been paroled and sent to the North.[73]

War in all of its worst manifestations visited Watauga County following the main thrust by Stoneman. Two Federal regiments under the command of Colonel George Kirk were ordered into the area, possibly passing through Banner Elk before arriving in Boone on April 5. Kirk established his headquarters in Boone at the Councill home, keeping just over four hundred men with him. On April 7, Major Andrew Bahney was ordered to take portions of the Second North Carolina Mounted Infantry to Deep Gap, while Major William Rollins took a portion of the Third North Carolina Mounted Infantry to Blowing Rock. Furthermore, Kirk was ordered to blockade both Sampson Gap and the Meat Camp Road. Boone, Deep Gap and Watauga Gap near Blowing Rock were all fortified. In Boone, Kirk ordered holes cut into the walls of the courthouse to provide firing ports, while three frame

This Deep Gap Highway Historical Marker is one of three marking the route of Stoneman's Raid. *Author's collection.*

dwelling houses and a log smoke house owned by John "Jack" Horton were dismantled and used to build a barricade around the courthouse. Ironically, Horton was a Unionist, but like his more Confederate-inclined neighbors, he was indiscriminately preyed on by the invaders. The stronghold in Deep Gap was "a palisade fort enclosing about an acre and ditched around." At Watauga Gap, the Federals also built works, possibly dismantling the summer home of Caldwell County resident James Harper, while at the same time cutting down trees to provide better observation points. The Federal soldiers named this work Fort Rollins, in honor of their major. These works were all constructed to help protect Stoneman's rear and keep open a line of retreat if it were needed.[74]

At least two temporary field hospitals were established in Watauga County to nurse sick Federal soldiers. Descendants recalled that the home of Ples and Margaret Welch in Deep Gap community was used by the Federals, with Margaret being forced to take care of Union soldiers who were infected with the measles. An undetermined structure in Boone was undoubtedly used as a field hospital. Five members of the Second North Carolina Mounted Infantry died while stationed there: William Bradley of typhoid on April 10, James Paine on April 11 of typhoid, John Maricle on April 15 of measles, Henry Evans on April 16 of typhoid and Robert Foster on April 22 of unknown causes. At least three of the men were buried in the slave section of the old Boone City Cemetery.[75]

Word quickly spread that the Federals were garrisoned in the area. People hurriedly began to hide what little food and few valuables that they still had after four years of hardship and war. Sally Brown, whose husband was in a prisoner-of-war camp in Maryland, started pulling the siding off her house and "crammed meat, grain, and dried food such as beans, dried fruits and vegetables between the walls, then nailed the boards back in place." Next, Brown put her good seed potatoes in the potato hole, covered them with straw and raked the bad potatoes on top. When the Federals did arrive, they found no meat and only rotten potatoes. The Lorenzo Ward family hid their meat under rocks, the same rocks the Federals sat upon when they came visiting their farm seeking provisions. Alfred Adams recalled concealing necessities "in hollow stumps in the woods, or digging holes in the ground to hide vegetables. We actually hid a yoke of oxen in a little ravine in a field behind some woods." At Joe Mast's gristmill along Cove Creek, his daughters took his horses into the woods and hid until the threat had passed. Mast himself slipped away, and the Federals took everything at the mill except one bag of ground meal that Mast's daughter Fronia hid by sitting on it and covering it with her skirt. It was often children sent to do the hiding, as a child or two from a large family would not be missed, even by home Yankees who knew the family. The David Greene family on Stony Fork Creek had a trapdoor in one room that led to a hidden cellar. The family kept their food in the cellar during the war.[76]

Since the majority of Kirk's men were from the area, and many had been hunted heavily by the home guard, their retribution on the local citizenry was vicious. They moved out in small bands to steal and "requisition" from the local population. "They came to our home every day to commandeer what they could find," recalled Alfred Adams. The home of Jonathan and Malinda Horton was robbed eighteen times in fourteen days. Sarah Johnson was out plowing "with an old scrawny horse" when the Federals arrived. The soldiers demanded that Mrs. Johnson unhitch the horse. She replied to their commander that "if he touched the horse she'd beat his brains out" with a hoe she was holding. After sizing up the situation, the Federal commander was rumored to have told his men to leave the horse, "because I'd have to kill the old fool and the horse ain't worth it." Even those who professed to be Union men were not immune to the ravages of Kirk's men. Rittenhouse Baird was out plowing when five Federal soldiers came and relieved him of his horse, saddle and bridle. Joshua Horton stated that he lost seven hundred pounds of bacon, fifty bushels of corn, twenty-five bushels of potatoes and thirty chickens, along with four thousand fence rails. William Vandyke lost one horse, possibly the one that Washington Shearer saw being ridden by a slave in Wilkesboro. John "Jack" Horton claimed not only losing the three houses and the smoke house that were used to fortify the courthouse in Boone but also a wagon jack, a harness, a mule, four saddles, seven stacks of hay, two wagons, twenty bushels of corn, three hundred pounds of bacon and a great deal of leather, not to mention fence rails taken and burned for the campfires of soldiers. Horton applied to the Federal government for reimbursement after the war, claiming $1553.20 in damages, but he was only awarded $512.00. Albert Wilson was at home when the raiders came through and recalled later that he "saw the houses of his neighbors burned and sacked."[77]

There were many happenstance meetings between local citizens and Federal soldiers. Alexander Elrod was taking a sack of corn to be milled when he encountered Federal cavalry. They ordered him to walk with them, and Elrod apprehensively agreed. However, "he walked very slowly, pretending to have rheumatism. He was soon placed on the horse of the last soldier who was unhappy with the added burden. This soldier lagged behind the column and finally ordered [Elrod] to dismount, hand over his sack of corn, and turn around. When [Elrod] realized that the expected shot had been intentionally fired over his head, he ran down the road very rapidly with no trace of rheumatism."[78]

Law and order soon completely broke down, though local citizens often tried to help one another. Malinda Horton, the wife of state senator Jonathan Horton, was reportedly robbed on Shearer's Hill, near the Three Forks Baptist Church. The robbers—John Ford, William Benton and John Rowland—apparently were not soldiers. They took her jewelry, but as she dismounted from her horse, she gave it a "lick with her riding whip" and the horse sped off. Sarah Hayes later spotted a brooch on the coat of one of the assailants, and when she asked him why he had it, he gave it to Miss Hayes, who returned it to Horton. On the other end of the county, three miles southeast of Zionville, Landrine Eggers was rumored to have amassed large amounts of gold. With no home guard left, a band from Tennessee determined to rob him. The family, learning of the plot, called on others to help. The robbers approached about daylight one morning, and within about thirty yards of the Eggers house, shots rang out, and one of the robbers fell dead, with another wounded. The robbers fled, leaving the dead man, "a young man named Madron." All day the Eggers family and their kin waited, and about dark, a woman approached the house and asked permission to remove the body, which was granted. The following day, two women and a boy brought a horse and sled and retrieved the body. These loved ones of the robbers were asked to pass along the message that the "defenders had not disbanded and to tell the gang to come again." Undoubtedly, scenes like the ones that befell the Hortons and Eggerses were repeated in every community in Watauga County.[79]

General Stoneman was back in Watauga County on April 17 with a large number of Confederate prisoners. One prisoner estimated the total number at over one thousand. Those prisoners were quartered in Blowing Rock for a night. At some point, several of them attempted to escape into an ivy (mountain laurel) thicket alongside the road. The guards fired on the band, a Captain Price of Virginia was badly wounded and he was left behind. Lieutenant John T. Shotwell also ran, and as he was attempting to surrender, Colonel Kirk was heard to say "D—n him, shoot him!" This order was carried out. "[T]his gallant young man was murdered right before our eyes and left lying as he had fallen," recalled a prisoner from Caldwell County. "A friend of his begged to be allowed to go to him and when permission was given, he went and straightened his body and took fifty dollars in gold, intending to send it to young Shotwell's father, but was soon relieved of it by an officer." The prisoners continued to Boone and possibly were quartered in the stockade built around the courthouse. One prisoner recalled, "Kirk rode into our midst, called us 'cowards, cut-throats, damned rebels,' and every vile thing he could think of, and threatened the most horrible vengeance if we attempted to escape." Stoneman spent the night with the Jordan Councill family once again. Whereas Stoneman had been kind to Mrs. Councill, due to the fact that she had often fed Federal prisoners at the jail in Boone, Kirk had kept the family locked in their rooms. Stoneman, "standing in the piazza and taking survey of what had once been a happy and beautiful home," now found "the fencing all gone, the gardens, shrubbery, and yard trampled bare, covered with raw hides of cattle and sheep, decaying carcasses, and all manner of filth." Stoneman left the following day, heading back into west Tennessee. His thousand prisoners moved to the west, camping the next night at the head of Cove Creek and the following night at Dugger's Forge in Carter County, Tennessee. Rations were not issued to the prisoners until they reached Greenville and were finally given hardtack and bacon. The majority of Stoneman's troops continued to raid toward the west. On April 23, Kirk received orders to move his command on toward Warm Springs and Asheville.[80]

The Confederacy quickly collapsed in April 1865. Robert E. Lee's Army of North Virginia was forced out of its entrenchments around Petersburg on April 2, 1865. The lines held by the Thirty-seventh Regiment, spread precariously thin, were the first to fall. Lee's army moved back toward the west in an attempt to turn south and link up with Confederates in North Carolina. However, the remnants of Lee's army were surrounded and compelled to surrender at Appomattox on April 9, 1865. Due to missing records, it is unclear just how many members of the First Cavalry received paroles due them. The records of the Thirty-seventh Regiment are a little better but still show fewer than ten Watauga County men in the ranks to receive those paroles. The Fifty-eighth Regiment and the remnants of the Army of Tennessee had moved from Alabama into South Carolina in February 1865. After the fall of Columbia, South Carolina, they moved into North Carolina and, in an effort to stave off the inevitable, fought portions of Sherman's army at Bentonville in March 1865. The Federals eventually won the battle, and the Confederates moved back west toward Greensboro. Confederate commander Joseph Johnston surrendered his command at the Bennett Place on April 26, 1865, and the men were paroled on May 2, 1865.

Thus the survivors, both the parolees from Appomattox and the Bennett Place, and those incarcerated in Federal prisons, began to make their way back home to Watauga County. David Baird, a lieutenant in the Fifty-eighth Regiment, was shot in the chest at the battle of Bentonville. He survived but was forced to ride in a wagon from Greensboro to Lenoir. When he reached Lenoir, his cousin, Eliza Baird, met the party with a horse. They traveled via the Globe community and up the mountain toward Valle Crucis. Eliza "kept both ears constantly alert for the saddle noises and conversations of riders who might be the dreaded criminals; each time she heard such sounds, she turned into the woods." They eventually made it home, and David survived. The family of fellow Fifty-eighth Regiment member John Cook recalled how the shoes had worn right off Cook's feet by the time he returned. Joseph Brown (First Cavalry) was captured on April 3, 1865, and imprisoned at Point Lookout, Maryland. He was released in late June and did not arrive home until late July. Captured with other home guard members, Tarleton Adams was imprisoned at Camp Chase in Ohio. He was sick when he was released, and it took him three months to get back to Watauga County, having to beg or steal to sustain himself along the route. "I'll never forget…when my little brother, Abner, and I spied a figure away down the road, so thin and tired, he was barely getting along," recalled Leah Adams Dougherty. It was Tarleton, "whom we had given up for dead. We ran to meet him, but he looked so thin and so unreal I just clung to his hand and cried…He was half starved and had walked hundreds of miles. He was only a boy, barely seventeen."[81]

In possibly the only surviving account of a local reaction to President Lincoln's assassination, Dougherty recalled seeing a Federal soldier ride down the road, toward the crowd of Federal soldiers milling about her home and yard. The Federals hurried toward the messenger, inquiring of his obviously important news. "When the courier came on down in calling distance, he shouted, 'Lincoln is killed.'" Dougherty rushed in to tell her mother, Betsy Adams, "who stopped for a few minutes before answering…'I don't know,' she said, 'I don't know…It may not be the best for the South.'" Mrs. Adams was correct; Lincoln's death was a blow to the South.[82]

"Thus ends the war between the two sections," Jonathan Miller (Fifty-eighth Regiment) wrote. The war had cost Watauga County dearly, with soldiers dead, farms destroyed and families damaged.[83]

Chapter 6

The Life of Watauga County's Johnny Rebs

Once the banquets were finished, the speeches given and the flags presented, Watauga County's sons rode and marched out of the mountains that they had called home. They were off on the "grand adventure" of their generation. Those first few volunteers probably believed that a handful of months and one glorious battle would be all that was necessary to secure Southern independence. Newton Greer (Thirty-seventh Regiment) recalled many years after the war, "You don't know anything about hard times unless you were in the Awful War."[84]

There were three periods of enlistment for Watauga County men entering into the Confederate army. The members of the first group, what became Company D, First North Carolina Cavalry, enlisted out of a sense of adventure and honor. Typically, these men joined in April, May, June and July 1861. After the battle of First Manassas in July 1861, many recognized that this was not going to be a short war, and another round of recruitment began. These recruits were usually a little older and married and enlisted out of a sense of honor and responsibility to their families and their communities. These men joined Companies B and E, Thirty-seventh North Carolina Troops. Lastly, with the eventual passage of the Conscription Act in 1862, another round of enlistment began. These men volunteered because they had to. By enlisting during the grace period, they were allowed to go into companies of their choosing, elect their own officers and receive a bounty. Those who waited until they were conscripted were placed into regiments of the government's choosing. Members of this third group became Companies D and I, Fifty-

The flag of the First North Carolina Cavalry was a variant of a standard Army of North Virginia battle flag. It resides in a private collection. *Author's collection.*

eighth North Carolina Troops. Company M of the Fifty-eighth was made up of conscripts from Watauga and Ashe Counties.

One nagging question remains: just why did these men fight? Since Watauga County seemingly had so little in common with the rest of North Carolina to the east, and the South as a whole, what propelled these men to take up arms voluntarily and fight? Unfortunately, very few of Watauga's sons left us their answers to that pivotal question. Harvey Davis (First Cavalry), in writing an introduction to his "Diary," did not "attempt to give any of the causes that led up to that Sanguinary conflict," outside of declaring that the war was an effort to "maintain their rights guaranteed by the constitution." Davis further chronicled that former General Assemblyman George Folk (First Cavalry) stood in the streets of Boone and spoke on "the attempt of the North to dominate the South and abrogate her rights under the Constitution." However, we must remember that Folk was a lawyer and politician, trying to persuade men to join his command. Jonathan Miller (Fifty-eighth Regiment) wrote many years after the conflict ended, "The war was gotten up by political schemers up North, with a view to obtain the reins of Government and to grow rich. A scheme in which they succeeded. Might often overcomes right...If the U.S. had decided to free the slaves, why did they not free them, and pay the owners, as England did?" Miller goes on, lamenting the cost of the war, stating that the cost "would have paid for all the slaves."[85]

After leaving Watauga, the men journeyed to a training camp. First, the Watauga Rangers went west to Asheville before heading east to Warren County, where the Rangers became Company D, First North Carolina Cavalry. Likewise, the Watauga Marksmen and the Watauga Minute Men also journeyed east. Their first assignment was Camp Fisher, near High Point. Once ten independent companies were in a training camp, they were authorized to form themselves into a regiment and to elect regimental commanders. On November 20, 1861, the Marksmen became Company B, and the Minute Men became Company E, Thirty-seventh North Carolina Troops. In mid-1862, Drewey Harmon and William Miller's companies initially went to Mitchell County and camped on the grounds of John B. Palmer's Grasslands Estate. On July 29, 1862, Harmon's Company became Company D, and Miller's Company became Company I, Fifty-eighth North Carolina Troops. The First Cavalry and the Thirty-seventh Regiment were on the way to Virginia not long after formation, while the Fifty-eighth Regiment was assigned to East Tennessee. A typical textbook regiment contained one thousand men in ten companies. The regiment was commanded by a colonel, assisted by a lieutenant colonel and major. They, along with an adjutant, a sergeant major, a quartermaster, a commissary, a surgeon, an assistant surgeon, field musicians and a chaplain, made up the field and staff of the regiment. The colonel, lieutenant colonel and major were elected by the company-grade officers, and the colonel was approved by the governor. A company had one hundred men under the command of a captain and two or three lieutenants. These were the company-grade officers who were elected by the men in the company. Noncommissioned officers (i.e., sergeants and corporals) were appointed from men in the ranks by the officers.

Above: The Horton brothers, Nathaniel and Jonathan, enlisted in Company A, First North Carolina Cavalry. Nathaniel (left) transferred to the Thirty-seventh, and Jonathan died in 1862 of "gastritis." *Courtesy Jenny Melville.*

Left: Captain William Young Farthing of the Thirty-seventh North Carolina Troops died of disease the same day his resignation was accepted. *Courtesy Cliff Farthing.*

If they wanted to leave the army, officers had the privilege of being able to resign their commissions. Captain Jonathan Horton (Thirty-seventh Regiment) resigned in July 1862, writing that he was "57 years old and my health is feeble, rendered so by the continued exposure of the service." His successor, Jordan Cook (Thirty-seventh Regiment), likewise resigned in November 1862, citing "the loss of sight" in one of his eyes. William Y. Farthing (Thirty-seventh Regiment) submitted his resignation on November 12, 1862, just two days after being declared exchanged. Farthing was captured at the battle of Hanover Court House, Virginia, the previous May. "I am fifty years old," Farthing wrote, "and have two sons; one of my sons is now a member of my co[mpany], and the other is about to enter the army, being subjected to the Conscript Law. I own no slaves, therefore my wife and daughters are left without any male assistance on the plantation." Farthing's resignation was accepted on November 28, 1862, the same day that he died in a hospital in Winchester, Virginia, of "pleuritis." Enlisted men did not have the luxury of resigning from service. Only death or a doctor's certificate could get them out of the army. Some soldiers went to great lengths to obtain a discharge though few were as creative as Keith Blalock, released from the Twenty-sixth North Carolina by reason of "hernia" and "poison from sumac," which he had given himself. Daniel Moretz was discharged in November 1862 by reason of "general dropsy and old age." He was in his mid-forties, hardly elderly.[86]

Once in camp, the soldiers slowly became acquainted with their new lives. Drill began, and the new recruits were issued arms. The Thirty-seventh Regiment was at first armed with antiquated flintlock muskets. In the spring of 1862, these were swapped for .69-caliber smoothbore muskets that had been converted from flintlocks to a percussion system of firing. It was not until after the battle of Chancellorsville, Virginia, in May 1863 that the Thirty-seventh regiment's men were armed with Enfield (.577 caliber) or Springfield (.58 caliber) rifles. The Fifty-eighth Regiment was also armed with .69 caliber smoothbore muskets until the summer of 1864, when they were swapped for .54-caliber Austrian Lorenz rifles, weapons brought over through the blockade. The First Cavalry was armed with pistols, shotguns, breech-loading Hall rifles and sabers. Also issued were cartridge boxes, cap boxes, bayonets and scabbards (for the infantrymen), waist belts and buckles, haversacks for carrying food, canteens, plates, cups and forks and knapsacks for extra clothing.

Men were recruited into the army for just one reason: to fight and win battles. Some battles were carefully planned, like Stonewall Jackson's flank

William Hartley, Thirty-seventh North Carolina Troops, was killed at the battle of Chancellorsville, Virginia, on May 3, 1863. *Courtesy Terry Harmon.*

attack at Chancellorsville in May 1863. Others happened quite by accident, like the first day of the battle of Gettysburg in July 1863. The cavalry was often on the flanks, skirmishing with the enemy cavalry, while infantry regiments lined up and battled it out at short distances. It usually took several months after formation before a regiment saw action. Harvey Davis (First Cavalry) joined in May 1861 and did not partake in combat until November 1861. The Thirty-seventh regiment was mustered into service in November 1861 and did not fight the Federals until March 1862. The members of the Fifty-eighth Regiment were in service for thirteen months, occasionally fighting in small groups against guerrillas in Kentucky and Tennessee, before their first big engagement at Chickamauga, Georgia, in September 1863.

Each man experienced combat differently. Some individuals were dismayed that they were being sent to take the life of another human. "A few," noted historian Bell Wiley, "abhorred the folly and wickedness of the impending destruction. Many thought fondly of homefolk—wives, sweethearts, parents, children, sisters, brothers—and hoped earnestly to be spared." While Christians often sought solace in prayer and meditation, sinners threw away their cards, forsaking, at least temporarily, their wicked ways. Almost all were nervous. Some joked; others tried to talk to their comrades. David Dugger (Thirty-seventh Regiment) first experienced combat at the battle of New Bern, North Carolina, in March 1862. Right before the battle began, he and another soldier were detailed back to camp to cook something to eat. Dugger told of his experiences many years later:

> *On the return* [to the company] *we had about a half dozen camp kettles full of peas. The kettles were strung on a pole, with George* [Lawrance] *at one end and I at the other. We had to go through a pine grove, and while going through there, we heard our first bomb shells, and we did not know what they were, and there we stood looking and wondering what on earth they could be as they went whizzing through the air. Presently one cut the top out of a pine, and then we found out what they were and forthwith proceeded to hug the earth without getting our arms around it. As soon as the sound of the shell died away we gathered our pole and started to the Fort. When we got there we had peas all over us, so that we could hardly be told from the peas.*[87]

Combat was often at close quarters, with a deafening noise and blinding and choking smoke. The long rifles that the soldiers carried were muzzle-loaders: a soldier had to retrieve a cartridge from his cartridge box, bite off the end of it and dump the powder down the barrel. The Minié ball was then inserted into the end of the gun, and the ramrod was used to push the bullet all the way to the breech of the weapon. Then, a percussion cap was placed on the cone of the weapon, the hammer pulled back and the trigger pulled. The hammer hit the cap, which exploded and sent a small flame into the breech of the rifle, which ignited the powder. Even with all these steps, a good soldier could fire three rounds a minute. Yet muskets and rifles soon became fouled and became harder to load. Soldiers had to either stop and clean their weapons or find a discarded rifle cleaner than their own. Peter Turnmire (Thirty-seventh Regiment) recalled that at one of the battles around Richmond, he had no holes in his clothing prior to the battle, but that evening, "I had 14 bullet holes in my clothes." Soldiers were often surrounded by families and friends in the companies where they served. In a short article written after the war, Turnmire described the battle of Gaines Mill, Virginia, in June 1862. "About one third of the regiment reached the top of the hill," wrote Turnmire,

This flag was issued to the Thirty-seventh North Carolina Troops in November or December 1862 and captured on April 2, 1865. *Courtesy Museum of the Confederacy.*

when the enemy poured a volley into the end of our regiment and we fell back to the foot of the hill. There we formed again and marched back up the hill in a file of four's and again they poured a volley into us and again we fell back to the foot of the hill and formed a line of battle and advanced to the top of the hill and dropped to our knees and began firing at the enemy and pretty soon it looked like the minie balls had trimmed all the bushes around us.

I [Peter W. Turnmire] *during the engagement, was standing between* [Thomas] *Hodge on the right and Vincent Greer on the left, a minie ball struck Hodge about the heart and I eased him down on the right and*

> *Vincent Greer was struck in the temple and I eased him down on my left. When the order was given for us to fall back for reinforcements, I did not hear the orders and Captain Horton came and slapped me on my back with a sword and said we were ordered to fall back. As we went down the hill where we formed in the morning, Riley Triplett's son, Calvin, went down the hill with us and a stray ball struck him in the heart and he pulled up his shirt bosom and said, "Look here! Capt. Horton, I'm killed," and fell back dead.*[88]

As the war evolved, so did the nature of combat. At first, the war resembled conflicts of the past in which long lines of troops battled each other out in the open. By 1863, and especially into 1864, the open fields were replaced by trenches. These frontline trenches were constructed of felled trees and dirt and often filled with mud or standing water. To raise a head above the trench invited death from a sharpshooter's rifle. Both the Thirty-seventh Regiment around Petersburg and Richmond in the east and the Fifty-eighth Regiment in the defenses around Atlanta in the west were involved in such warfare. Daniel Carlton (First State Troops) recorded in his diary the fighting at the battle of the Wilderness. "May 5th/64…Formed line of battle to the left of the pike road about 1 o'clock p.m. Advanced on the enemy and gave them considerable bout capturing 2 piece of artillery and about 2,000 prisoners. Considerable casualties in the Regt. Threw up breastworks and lay in line of battle all night. fighting along the line at intervals all the night."[89]

During the war, the Confederate government sought to honor those soldiers who had performed above and beyond the call of duty during combat. While the government wanted to issue medals, the limited supply of resources prevented their distribution. Instead, Confederate officials ordered that once the individual companies had chosen among themselves, the list, a "Roll of Honor," was to be read at the next dress parade and published in local newspapers. Following the battle of Chancellorsville in May 1863, the two local companies in the Thirty-seventh nominated Sergeant Joel Fairchild and Private John E. Coffey. After the battle of Chickamauga, Georgia, in September 1863, the local men in the Fifty-eighth North Carolina nominated Private Braxton Cox and Sergeant John Eggers. It appears that the practice fell out of favor soon thereafter and was not continued.

Men from Watauga were involved in some of the costliest actions of the war, battles that produced ghastly wounds. Muskets and rifles placed in the hands of the soldiers fired soft lead projectiles that traveled at low velocities. When the bullet struck an arm or leg, the bone shattered. Amputation was

These images most likely depict (from left to right) Jordan Cook, A.J. Critcher and Thomas D. Cook, all elected as lieutenants in Company B, Thirty-seventh North Carolina Troops, on September 14, 1861. The sword and pistol are probably photographer's props. *Author's collection.*

the only available treatment, and medical wisdom of the time believed that for a soldier to recover, surgery needed to be performed within twenty-four hours. Wesley Presnell (Fifty-eighth Regiment) lost his left arm following the battle of Rocky Face Ridge, Georgia, in February 1864. Artillery pieces fired both solid shot and hollow rounds that were meant to explode, providing the fuse was good. When infantry and cavalry were within short range, artillerymen switched to canister, and the cannons became large shotguns. Artillery rounds likewise produced serious wounds, though fewer than those inflicted by muskets. Bugler Smith Carroll (First Cavalry) was struck in the thigh by shell fragments in a skirmish near Culpepper Court House in September 1863. He was captured, and the Federal surgeon amputated his leg right there on the field. Carroll survived. Smith Holeman (Fifty-eighth Regiment) was wounded at a battle near the Chattahoochee River, Georgia, on July 10, 1864. His arm was amputated, but gangrene infected the wound, and he died in a hospital a month later. Artillery also caused less noticeable though equally severe injuries. George W. Cable (Thirty-seventh Regiment) was injured by a shell "which destroyed his hearing" at the battle of Second Manassas, Virginia, August 29, 1862.[90]

To treat the expected injuries, when commanders knew that a battle was imminent, they would often direct their surgeons to establish field hospitals to the rear of the fighting, sometimes a mile or more to the rear. Surgeons from different regiments formed brigade hospitals, while assistant surgeons went out to evaluate wounded soldiers near the front lines. Those men who

John Ward, Thirty-seventh North Carolina Troops, later died of wounds he received at the battle of Gaines Mill, Virginia, in June 1862. *Courtesy Terry Harmon.*

were wounded and could walk were directed to field hospitals. Men who were seriously wounded had to wait for friends or someone with a stretcher to bear them off the field. At times, they had to wait hours or even days to receive care. Field hospitals presented the truest horrors of war. Medical stores were often in short supply. Men who had been wounded in every conceivable way were placed on the ground, awaiting their turn with the surgeons. Sergeant Calvin Cottrell (Fifty-eighth Regiment) was wounded at the battle of Resaca, Georgia, his "right eye shot out destroying also the nasal bone." Wesley Presnell (Fifty-eighth Regiment) lost an arm that same month. The wound that William Randall (Thirty-seventh Regiment) sustained in June 1862 in the left shoulder deprived "him of the use of his left arm" and got him discharged from the army. Elijah Norris (Fifty-eighth Regiment) wrote a postwar article recalling his wounding in Georgia: "On that day just as the sun was setting, I was shot down, and thought I was killed, a big bullet lacking only about an inch of going through me. This was on September 4 [1864], one day before I was 21 years old. They took me to a hospital where I stayed until sometime in November."[91]

Many soldiers died in the field hospitals, either while awaiting treatment or in spite of the efforts of those caring for the wounded. Soldiers able to return to the ranks did so, while the more seriously wounded were transferred via railroads to more permanent hospital facilities. These were often in large cities like Atlanta and Macon, Georgia; or Richmond, Petersburg, Winchester and Lynchburg, Virginia. Chimborazo Hospital in Richmond was the largest, North or South. Over 77,889 patients passed through this hospital during the war. At these facilities, the care was better, but medical supplies were often in short supply. Some soldiers survived despite grievous wounds. James Parlier (Twenty-sixth Regiment) was a school teacher in Watauga County before the war. "I have bin at hospitle parte of the time," he wrote home to his brother in January 1865, "and had a ball cut out of my hand it was lodged against the bones in the back of my hand. It near made me twist my tale when the doctors was cuting it out but it is nearly healed up." The family of Wyatt Hayes (Thirty-seventh Regiment) recalled this story about his wounding and recovery:

> *The first day of the Seven Days Battle around Richmond a "minnie ball" tore away the front of his left foot. He lay on the battlefield until dark after which he was taken to a field hospital tent and the mangled front of his foot was amputated...One night he awoke to terrible pain and blood all around. When help came, they discovered a fly had gotten to his wounded foot as he lay on the battlefield and deposited eggs on the wound. Now they had hatched and maggots had eaten through the sutures of the blood vessels and he was bleeding badly.*
>
> *The nurses poured on medication to make the maggots roll out and then re-sutured the foot. After he began to improve...*[92]

At times, wounded and sick soldiers were furloughed and allowed to return home. As they traveled via train from Virginia or Georgia toward the mountains, they could stop at one of the many wayside hospitals to eat and get their wounds dressed. The wayside hospital in Salisbury reported that between July 14, 1862, and April 1, 1863, the facility treated 1,235 soldiers, including 19 from Watauga. There were undoubtedly many more receiving care over the coming months.[93]

Calculating the actual losses during the war is difficult. Somewhere between 620,000 and 700,000 men died. Only 205,000 deaths are attributed to battlefield action. The other 400,000 or more are men who died of disease. The soldiers from Watauga County were just as susceptible as men from other areas. The first Watauga County resident to die during the war appears to be Private Edmund Miller (First Cavalry), a nineteen-year-old Meat Camp resident who succumbed to pneumonia on November 24, 1861, in camp near Centerville, Virginia. There were scores of men from Watauga for whom no cause of death was listed, or whose records simply say "disease," "fever" or "sickness." At least fifteen men from Watauga County died of typhoid fever, usually contracted through drinking water that had been contaminated with feces. Typhoid usually produces a fever, along with diarrhea. Chronic diarrhea is listed as killing sixteen men from Watauga

William Greene, Thirty-seventh North Carolina Troops, died of disease in January 1862. *Courtesy Sheree Sloop.*

County, but they could have also had typhoid, as the conditions frequently occurred in tandem. At least ten Watauga County soldiers died of pneumonia. Often, pneumonia was a complication of some other disease, like typhoid, bronchitis, a simple cold or the measles.

Common childhood diseases ran rampant through the camps in 1861 and 1862. "We had about forty in the hospital a few weeks ago," wrote Barzilla McBride (First Cavalry) in November 1861. A couple of weeks later, he wrote, "The health of our regiment is very good this time with the exception of some Chicken Pox which is very annoying to us. The first excitement was that it was small pox but we have ascertained that it is nothing but chicken pox." James Tugman (Thirty-seventh Regiment) wrote home in February 1862: "there is some sickness in our regiment at this time some mumps yet and janders [jaundice] and other complaints." Sickness was especially bad in the Fifty-eighth Regiment in the winter of 1862–63. The men were stationed around Jacksboro in east Tennessee. George W. McGuire wrote on December 18, 1862, "There is a heap of sickness heare in camp is not half of our company that is able for duty." Jonathan Miller wrote that the Fifty-eighth "suffered severely from privation and exposure which was the cause of many deaths by Pneumonia and relapse of measles." There could also have been something wrong with the water, but what exactly made hundreds of men sick that winter remains a mystery. Regardless, about one hundred of them died and are buried at the Delap Family Cemetery in Campbell County, Tennessee. Once the men had been in service for a while, their immunity systems toughened to the diseases of camp. However, whenever new recruits arrived, they were susceptible to the same common diseases to which many of them had never before been exposed.[94]

While some soldiers were discharged from the army due to their inability to perform their duties, others were simply transferred to the Invalid Corps.

Established in early 1864, the Invalid Corps had members who served as guards and clerks because they were no longer able to withstand service in combat regiments. George W. Cable (Thirty-seventh Regiment), Harvey Davis (First Cavalry), Thomas B. Farthing (First Cavalry), James Proffitt (First Cavalry) and Joseph C. Shull (Thirty-seventh Regiment) were all transferred from their regiments to the Invalid Corps. Farthing actually served as a nurse in one of the hospitals in Richmond. While Invalid Corps members could return to front-line duty if they regained full health, there is little evidence to support that such transfers really happened.

Adjusting to camp life took a great deal of time. Once the soldiers arrived in camp, there were many obstacles to overcome. The men who became Confederate soldiers had always lived independently, making their own choices in life. Now, someone or something regulated their entire lives, telling them when to rise, sleep and eat. The Thirty-seventh Regiment was stationed at Camp Mangum in January 1862. A Tar Heel soldier recorded this daily schedule in April 1862:

> *Reveille At Daybreak*
> *Breakfast call at 6 1/2 a.m.*
> *Sick call at 7 a.m.*
> *Guard-Mounting at 730 a.m.*
> *Squad Drill from 8 to 9 a.m.*
> *Company Drill from 10 to 12 m.*
> *Orderly call 12 m.*
> *Dinner call at 12 1/2 p.m.*
> *Battalion Drill from 3 to 430 p.m.*
> *Dress Parade at 530 p.m.*
> *Tattoo at 8 p.m.*
> *Taps at 830 p.m.*[95]

Either the drum and fife or a bugle signaled Reveille each morning. Calvin Miller (Thirty-seventh Regiment) and Lorenzo Miller and Jesse Keller (Fifty-eighth Regiment) all served as fifers; Samuel Swift (Thirty-seventh Regiment), who died of chronic diarrhea in 1864, was a drummer. William Kilby and Cornelius Carlton (Fifty-eighth Regiment) are both listed simply as musicians. While some drummers were truly boys, most were in their mid-twenties. Drummer Swift was thirty years old when he enlisted. The drummers often called the men to the sick call and fatigue duty and, while the troops were on the march and drill fields, beat the cadence.[96]

Luther Penley served as a private in Company B, Thirty-seventh North Carolina Troops, and died in Virginia in July 1862 of unknown causes. *Courtesy Greg Mast.*

"We have to drill twice a day 2 hours of a morning and 2 in the evening," recorded Silas McBride (Thirty-seventh Regiment). These drills were more than just a way to occupy the soldiers' time. They taught them how to move in the formations dictated by the training manuals of the day. A line of battle consisted of a long line of two ranks, facing the enemy. On the march, the men formed a column of fours, shortening the line. The men were taught to march by the left or right flank, how to move around obstacles, deploy as skirmishers, move in quick time toward the enemy and seemingly countless other maneuvers.[97]

Very few soldiers liked guard or picket duty. In the infantry, every few days, a certain number of men from each regiment were detailed to stand along a picket line and watch for the enemy. These pickets were marched out of camp to a location near enemy lines. In the early days of the war, they stood out in the open or along a river watching for the opposing forces to move. Jonathan Miller (Fifty-eighth Regiment) found the "guard duty at Big Creek Gap were excessive, and the command suffered severely," while his regiment was in east Tennessee the winter of 1862–63. Daniel Carlton (First State Troops) chronicled in his diary in April 1864 of being sent out "on picket at 7 o'clock a.m. marched 9 miles to old picket ground, and 80 men of our regt. went on post. commenced snowing at 12 m. At one commenced raining, rained all day." In mid-1864, the nature of the war changed. Picket posts were located in pits in front of the entrenchments around Petersburg and Richmond in Virginia and at Atlanta in Georgia. Pickets were changed under the cover of darkness and were vulnerable to frequent capture. For the Watauga County men serving in the First North Carolina Cavalry, picket duty was little different. Cavalrymen were almost always on picket duty, serving on the flanks of the army, watching for enemy movements. Harvey Davis recalled that picket duty was "the most difficult and hard task of a soldier. Being compelled to stand 2 hours of each 6 hours on picket alone in the most dismal storms of cold snow rain hail or sleet often miles from the camp & expecting the enemy any moment tried the courage of the stoutest…many was the poor solder who bit the dust while thus serving as the eye of the army by being stealthly approached in the dark and cut down before he knew of the danger."[98]

Soldiers not on guard duty, sick in the hospital or on the drill field still faced a host of distressing issues. All soldiers wanted the war to end so that they could permanently go back home to their loved ones. Many realized that was not going to happen in the immediate future. So the next best thing was to get a furlough home. A furlough was a slip of paper that was signed by the commanding officer of the regiment. Soldiers needed the furlough to leave camp. Simply going to town for an afternoon required a furlough. But the coveted ones allowed the bearer to return home. They were often granted for ten, twenty or thirty days. A soldier in Virginia on furlough could have taken a train to present-day Hickory, where he would have then started walking. If he was lucky, he might hitch a ride with a farmer heading in his same direction. On several occasions, James M. Tugman (Thirty-seventh Regiment) wrote home, mentioning a desire to come home. "I should like to see you but I cannot have the opportunity…to come [before] spring," he wrote in one letter. Often, soldiers who had been wounded or who were sick were given furloughs to go home and recuperate. Occasionally, there were family or friends from home visiting the troops. At other times, soldiers visited friends in other regiments. Daniel Carlton (First State Troops) wrote in his diary in May 1864 about going to see his brothers in different regiments in the midst of the Overland Campaign.[99]

In addition to homesickness, another vexing problem was getting paid. Confederate privates received $11 a month until June 1864, when they received a $7 raise. Corporals received $13, and second through fifth sergeants received $17, while first (sometimes called orderly) sergeants received $20. Second lieutenants received $80, first lieutenants $90, captains $130, majors $150, lieutenant colonels $170 and colonels $195. Soldiers were mustered for pay every two months. The officers of a company labored for several days on company muster roll sheets, documenting the soldier and what, if any, charges he had incurred during the previous two months. Soldiers could be docked for wasting cartridges or losing equipment. A soldier convicted of being absent without leave could have his pay docked for the time absent. Such were the cases of John S. Farthing and Eli Farthing (Thirty-seventh Regiment). Save for the spring and summer of 1862, the Watauga County men in the Thirty-seventh Regiment and the First Cavalry were paid regularly. The local men in the Army of Tennessee had a harder time of it and frequently went months on end without receiving pay. Toward the end of the war, a portion of the Confederate treasury was entrusted to Army of Tennessee commander General Joseph E. Johnston. He used portions of this, Mexican silver dollars, to pay his men one final time before the war ended. What little money a soldier had was often sent home, usually transported by a fellow soldier already headed in that direction. Inflation affected the soldiers in the army just as it did the people back at home. "[E]verything is high here we have to pay Double the rate," Silas Green wrote in January 1862.[100]

An additional problem was the level of conflict sometimes present between officers and enlisted men. Twenty-four of the thirty-two men who became officers were, according to the 1860 census, in the middle and upper classes prior to the war. Most were farmers, while James W. Councill (First Cavalry) was a blacksmith, Joseph B. Todd (First Cavalry) was the clerk of court, Jordan C. McGee (Fifty-eighth Regiment) was a brick mason, Albert F. Davis (Fifty-eighth Regiment) was a teacher and Drewey Harmon (Fifty-eighth Regiment) was a minister. Most soldiers in the ranks were in the lower economic brackets and had a variety of reactions to their leadership. "We have splendid officers in our regiment they are very strict," wrote Barzilla C. McBride (First Cavalry) in August 1861. Of course, officers, as well as attitudes, changed as the war went on. McBride's first captain, George Folk, resigned in May 1862 and was replaced by Lieutenant John C. Blair. Commenting on the number of deserters leaving his regiment in the spring of 1863, McBride wrote that he "would not be surprised if many more left for Blair is not fit to be captain of any thing." Bennett Smith (Thirty-seventh Regiment) informed his wife back at home in March 1862 that he was "going to tri to git a long with the officers the best I can tel my time is out then I will say what I think[.]"[101]

For a host of reasons, mostly undefined, some soldiers sought transfers from their regiments to others. Some transfers likely were the result of a soldier wanting to be closer to family members. Anderson Cable transferred from the Eighteenth North Carolina Regiment to the Thirty-seventh Regiment in late 1864. Cornelius Carlton moved from the Thirty-seventh Regiment to the Fifty-eighth Regiment in February 1863.

If there was one subject equally as important to the soldiers as family and furloughs home, it was food. The Confederate army was supposed to supply rations to its troops: beef or pork, hard bread and vegetables to each soldier; and beans, rice or hominy, coffee, sugar, salt and vinegar to each company. But food always seemed to be in short supply. Bennett Smith (Thirty-seventh Regiment) wrote home in March 1862: "As to eatables we have little a plenty Hit is some flour corne meal about haf sifted [and] some rise shugar and pork Beef the beef is damaged so we can hardly eat it." A couple of months later, Silas Green (Thirty-seventh Regiment) wrote, "We have plenty to eat Such as it is flour Bread and Beef and Bacon Rice and a little sugar We Dont get any Coffey." While many imagine hardtack, the square cracker mentioned in the manuals of the time, as synonymous with military service, Confederate soldiers were rarely issued hardtack. Instead, they were issued cornmeal or baked bread. As the war progressed, rations were often cut. Jonathan Miller (Fifty-eighth Regiment) recalled that after Atlanta fell and the Confederate army moved north toward Tennessee, the men were issued "less than half ration…[and] were compelled to make their ration for the day following by parching corn which continued all night, each mess taking turns, keeping the pans hot all night." Walter Story (Fifty-eighth Regiment) complained in November 1863, "We get a little beef and a little bread, not half enough. I would be glad to eat what you threw away." The men often formed messes to help with camp chores. "I expect you would like to no how we manage a bout cooking there is fifteen of us messes together [and] that number a lowes us a cook that keeps one man from drilling while he is cooking I dont cook any I fetch water sometimes [and] make a fire [and] the rest cooks," recorded Bennett Smith (Thirty-seventh Regiment). Jordan S. Councill (Thirty-seventh Regiment) recorded in February 1862 that his messmates included Will Danner, Franklin Cozzens, William Henry Cozzens, David Cook, Joshua Cook, Sidney Holder, Jackson and Joseph Benfield, Jesse Brown, Jordan D. Councill and Charles Davis, "and I like them all very well," he added. Interestingly, since the Cozzens brothers were poor and free men of color, Councill's list indicates that the mess organization, at least in this case, crossed economic and racial boundaries.[102]

Food distribution was disrupted once active campaigning began. Harvey Davis (First Cavalry) recalled being given just fifteen minutes to prepare three days' worth of rations in July 1862. It was common to be given three days' rations on the start of a march. Soldiers usually spent the evening preparing those rations. Each soldier was issued a haversack to carry his rations, but many soldiers would just eat all three days' rations at once, preferring to carry them in their stomachs instead of in a sack. Occasionally, while on the march, soldiers were given a ration of whiskey. John W. Dugger (Fifty-eighth Regiment) wrote of getting a whiskey ration twice during active campaigning in the spring and summer of 1864. Hungry soldiers would often resort to activities loved ones back home might question. After the war, Newton Greer (Thirty-seventh Regiment) recalled "eating molded corn bread taken from a dead soldiers knapsack" once during a campaign. He went on to describe how "once when they were marching from one place to another, they came upon a spot where a cow had been slaughtered. They took what was left, the feet, made a fire and put on a pot of water to boil them. Before they were cooked, they were told to march away. One soldier was so hungry that he reached into the boiling water with his bare hands to get a cow foot and received a serious burn."[103]

Soldiers supplemented their rations whenever and however possible. In some instances, soldiers could purchase food from sutlers, civilian merchants authorized to sell goods like stationery, books and food to soldiers. At times, soldiers could go into the countryside and beg or buy extra food. William H. Horton (Fifty-eighth Regiment) was detailed away from his regiment to drive a herd of mules as the Army of Tennessee struck out from Atlanta in the fall of 1864. After complaining about the small amount of beef and cornmeal he was drawing, he added, "We can buy Sweet potatoes and git some pumpkins and we can buy flour and we can sorter make out to live but it is a hard life." A month later, Horton wrote home that he was running out of money. Writing from eastern North Carolina in mid-1864, James W. Horton (Sixth Cavalry) told family back in Watauga County that his companions were healthy, since "we can steel as many watermeleons as we want. So the 6 cav. will not starve." Harvey Davis (First Cavalry) was lucky enough to participate in a raid on a group of Federal wagons bearing a load of sutler stores right before Christmas 1862. "[T]here were lots of fine delicacies for Christmas," he wrote. "It was unusual to see our men making Rio coffee and eating fine cake, chees[e], oranges, lemons, and nuts of all kinds and strutting in fine yankee boots."[104]

Often, soldiers wrote home with their culinary wants and wishes. Bennett Smith (Thirty-seventh Regiment) wrote frequently to his wife, Jane, about what he wanted her to send. In February 1863, he asked for dried fruit and a cake of sugar. A month later, Smith wrote thanking his wife for the provisions she had sent. "Jiney I can inform you," he wrote, "that I got the box of provision you sent to me...their was nothing hurt of any count their was a few of the Eggs broak [and] Som of the taters had froaz the rest

Thomas Jefferson Coffey taught school in Valle Crucis prior to enlisting in the Fifty-eighth North Carolina Troops. *Courtesy Caldwell Heritage Museum.*

of the victuals was awl Sound." Sometimes these boxes from home were transported to camp by a soldier returning from leave; at other times, a local man in a community, often a father of a soldier, might transport a wagonload of boxes to the nearest railhead and see them safely to the army. Evidently, they were in good hands with only a few broken eggs.[105]

Letters home were the lifelines for many a soldier. "Dear Father Mother Brother [and] Sisters," wrote James Tugman (Thirty-seventh Regiment) in an undated letter. "I seat myself this morning to drop you a few lines to let you know that I am well and all satisfied and I hope these few lines comes to hand they may find you as well." Tugman's introduction was a standard turn of phrase common to the time period. "I hardly no what to rite," words penned by Bennett Smith (Thirty-seventh Regiment) in February 1862, also comprised a common phrase. William H. Horton (Fifty-eighth Regiment) told his family, "We hear so many tails a bout [the war] that I cant rite any thing a bout it." However, Smith and others who sent letters home did seem to know what to write. They informed their loved ones of who was sick, who had died, their experiences in battle and on the march and the mundane activities associated with camp life. More interesting to the soldiers away fighting the war were the happenings back at home. "They was nothing on top of this Green Earth that gave me more satisfaction than to here from you," wrote Jordan S. Councill (Thirty-seventh Regiment) in January 1862. Silas Green (Thirty-seventh Regiment) wrote his family, asking them to write to him and to let him "know how all the Cove Creek people is getting along." Echoing Green, Barzilla McBride (First Cavalry) wrote asking "any body and everybody, that feel disposed to write and I will receive them gladly." Letters home could be sent via the regular postal system. There were post offices, often in a home or store, in Blowing Rock, Boone, Meat Camp, Mortez Mill, Rotherwood, Stony Fork, Sugar Grove, Sweet Water, Valle Montis, Valle Crucis and Watauga Falls. The letters had to be stamped or "franked." However, a much more reliable means of getting letters between the army and home was by asking the countless individuals on their way between the two. Smith wrote a letter in February 1863 to his wife, Jane, stating that he had just written a letter, but since Captain Critcher was on his way back to Watauga County, this letter "would be Shore to go." George Adams (First Cavalry) wrote in January 1862 that he was taking letters back home. Many a letter was quickly drafted and stuffed in a jacket pocket when a comrade was leaving camp.[106]

"Their is awl sorts of amusements going on hear," Bennett Smith (Thirty-seventh Regiment) recorded in a letter home from camp in 1862: "fidling dancing plaing bast bool pen jumping rasling and a heap of other things [and] some of the wickeds men you ever saw and the ugyes that you evr heard tel of." Actually fighting battles took a small percentage of a soldier's time, and drill, along with the other normal routines of camp life, only consumed so many hours of a day. The common soldier could frequently find time to play games, gamble, read and a host of other activities. Examining Smith's letter, we find "Fidling [and] dancing"; for those religiously inclined, playing the fiddle and dancing were frowned upon. But the evening hours could often find the soldiers gathered around a campfire with someone sawing out a tune on a fiddle. Some regiments even had informal string bands with fiddles, guitars and banjos. Popular Southern war songs included "Bonnie Blue Flag," "Stonewall Jackson's Way" and "Richmond is a Hard Road to Travel." Minstrel tunes were also common, songs like the beloved "Dixie's Land." Other songs were carryovers from those heard back at home, like "Cumberland Gap" and "Wait for the Wagon," while others were sentimental parlor tunes, like "Weeping Sad and Lonely," "Do they Miss Me at Home" and "Somebody's Darling." The song "Home, Sweet Home," moved so powerfully on the soldiers that it was frequently banned by officers.[107]

Calvin Miller of the Thirty-seventh North Carolina Troops was one of just a handful of Watauga County men to serve as musicians during the war. *Courtesy John Hawkins.*

Undoubtedly, "plaing bast bool" was the game of baseball, a sport that became widely popular during the war but was not yet defined by a strict set of rules. While there would have been a ball and bat, there could have been two, three or four bases. And to be considered out, players had to be actually struck by the ball. Soldiers generally played other games as well, including "foot racing, wrestling [Smith's 'rasling'], boxing, leapfrog, hopscotch, quoits, and marbles," according to historian Bell Wiley. Soldiers also fished and came up with ingenious ways to hunt without using firearms. William Horton (Fifty-eighth Regiment) painted yet a different portrait of camp life, writing to his sister in late 1862, "This company is the worst Co to swear and gambel you ever seen in your life. They play Cards day and night." Card games, such as poker, twenty-one, euchre and keno, were common among some of the soldiers, and frequently a soldier's entire pay could be wiped out quickly if he were unlucky in games of chance.[108]

Bennett Smith also told his wife in another 1862 letter, "It is a gainst the ruils for the soldiers to use any profain langueg but it its don a greait deal there is a heap of mean men here." A few resorted to taking from others. Newton Greer (Thirty-seventh Regiment) later recalled a man in his company "who took a pair of underwear off a clothes lines as they were marching by. The lady of the house yelled, 'You'll pay at Judgment Day.' He said 'If I've got that long, I'll take another pair.' He did."[109]

Many of those "mean men" whom Smith mentioned would pay sooner, eventually running afoul of the military justice system. When a soldier was mustered into service, he was read the Articles of War. There were 101 articles that governed, or regulated, the armies, both North and South. According to Article 3, a soldier could be fined one dollar for each "profane oath or execration" that escaped from the lips; for speaking against the president, vice president or members of Congress, an officer could be cashiered and an enlisted man court-martialed. Article 23 stated that any officer or enlisted soldier who "advised or persuaded any other officer or soldier to desert" could be executed or punished, "as shall be inflicted upon him by sentence of a court-martial." Likewise, a soldier who deserted could also be executed or punished accordingly. Most court-martials were held within the regiment, with officers serving as judges and attorneys. While the actual proceedings of court-martials did not survive the fires that engulfed Richmond as the war ended, we do know that at least thirty-five local soldiers were tried for a variety of offenses during the war. Most were related to being absent without leave or deserting. For some, the punishment was simply some type of camp confinement. Barzilla McBride (First Cavalry) recalled in a letter home that the "men dig stumps as a form of punishment." Jordan S. Councill (Thirty-seventh Regiment) was reported absent without leave from July to October 1863. He returned to duty in November and was court-martialed on November 11, 1863, and ordered to perform "company punishment." Councill wrote home on January 17, 1864, "My punishment was read at...the 6th of this month instant to wear a ball and chain 3 months and do police duty 4 [hours] each day and forfit pay that is due to the last day of february 1864. Well my dear I dont care a dam for the money for it is not no count no how but the other is what I dread...I dont intend to do any dutey while I ware it I will see them in hell first and tell you if they force it on me I do done fiten that is shore."[110]

For other soldiers, the punishment was much more severe. William Carroll (First Cavalry) deserted May 1, 1863. He was arrested, tried and convicted of being a thief and confined to Salisbury Prison until December 1, 1864. On several occasions, the death penalty was prescribed for deserters. James S. Greer (Thirty-seventh Regiment) came up missing after the battle of Fredericksburg, Virginia, in December 1862. He was later declared a deserter, brought back under guard and, after a trial, executed on an unknown date. Lewis Orrant (Thirty-seventh Regiment) was also court-martialed for desertion. Orrant, like Greer, was found guilty and sentenced to death, but for an unknown reason, his sentence was never actually carried out. Michael Ward (Fifty-eighth Regiment) joined in July 1862, deserted in October 1862 but returned in June 1863. He deserted a second time in August 1863 but was reported as being present but under arrest. Ward was married and had three children back in Watauga County. He was court-martialed on April 4, 1864, and sentenced to be executed on May 4. There were actually twelve members of the Fifty-eighth Regiment executed on May 4 in the Crow Valley just north of Dalton, Georgia. The condemned men were transported to the area in a wagon, while their brigade, including the Fifty-eighth Regiment, was drawn up into a hollow square. After the condemned men were blindfolded and tied to stakes, the firing squad was lined up about thirty feet away. A portion of the firing squad's weapons were loaded with blank rounds, and the squad did not know who had the live rounds. At noon, the order was given to fire. "O! what a [day] was that!" the assistant surgeon of the Sixtieth North Carolina Troops wrote. "The private soldiers were all bitterly opposed to the executions of these men…I can never, never forget that sad scene; I was heart sick." After the men were executed, the entire brigade marched by the dead men before they were buried. This was done to serve as an example to men who contemplated desertion.[111]

Not all the men in the army were troublemakers or even the "mean men" that Smith mentioned in his letter home. And a few of those men might have even changed their ways during the war years. Large revivals swept through the armies, especially during the winter months when active campaigning had come to a close. In his diary, Daniel Carlton (First State Troops) mentioned going frequently to preaching. Sometimes the services were held in the mornings and at other times in the evening. On April 17, 1864, Carlton noted, "At 3 o'clock, p.m. the Baptism of 7 soldiers took place in a small creek by [the chaplain]." Two years earlier, Bennett Smith (Thirty-seventh Regiment) noted that they were having "preaching here evry few dayes he is able precher I go evry time to meting." This trend continued throughout the war, even though at times, there was a shortage of chaplains and missionaries working within the regiments.[112]

While the missionaries and chaplains who were available likely taught the value of forgiveness, there are few surviving examples that show how the Confederates from Watauga County viewed their foes across the battle lines. And those few references that do survive are all from early in the war. Harvey

These are the surviving remnants of two different flags carried by the Fifty-eighth North Carolina Troops. *Courtesy North Carolina Museum of History.*

Davis (First Cavalry) recorded in his diary November 25, 1861, as the date of a small skirmish in which he was involved, seeing for the first time "wild yankees." In an undated letter to John Eggers, Barzilla C. Green (Thirty-seventh Regiment) recorded that he had seen "three yankee prisoners the other day they ant so might big." Barzilla McBride wrote in September 1861 that he had volunteered to "kill yankees." There is, however, nothing to really show a changing attitude, save silence, in surviving correspondence. As the war continued, it appears that the novelty began to wane, and the soldiers were more concerned about their families and their own needs.[113]

Considering the almost one thousand men (and one woman) who served, mostly in the Confederate army during the Civil War, the surviving correspondence, diaries and reminiscences are few. However, the extracts here give glimpses into the lives of the men who left Watauga County and fought in both the Army of Northern Virginia and the Army of Tennessee.

Chapter 7

Reconstruction

Lee's surrender in Virginia, in conjunction with Johnston's surrender near Durham, marks a convenient place to end the narrative about the war proper. However, the war actually continued for years in the mountains of western North Carolina. William Cook (Fifty-eighth Regiment), as he was passing through Lenoir, was told "not to go to home; that the bushwhackers were in the woods in great numbers and were stealing, robbing, and carrying off everything they could get." Cook's mother "sent him to a pine thicket, and to that place she would make a daily pilgrimage, carrying him things to eat." Later he confessed, "I was so discouraged I went out in the thicket and wept."[114]

Information about Reconstruction in Watauga County is sparse. On April 28, 1865, the war was declared over in North Carolina. Governor Vance was arrested on May 13, and on May 29, President Andrew Johnson, who had replaced the assassinated Abraham Lincoln, appointed William Holden as North Carolina's governor and granted amnesty to all former Confederate soldiers, save those who fell into one of fourteen classes. Included in those fourteen were anyone who had held the rank of colonel or above, possessed $20,000 or more in personal or real wealth in 1860 or had been an elected or appointed Confederate official; these men had to write to the president, formally requesting to be pardoned. There were only four applications sent from Watauga: Hugh Dobbin, postmaster at Elk Cross Roads; Silas Morphew, postmaster at Rotherwood; Elijah Tatum, postmaster at Moretz's Mill; and, Henry Taylor, postmaster at Valle Crucis, who also served as the tax collector. All four were not pardoned until May 1866.[115]

Despite the many regulations that accompanied Reconstruction, or perhaps because of them, there was much lawlessness in the mountains. A gang based out of a Wilkes County home known as "Fort Hamby" plagued citizens in the surrounding counties. This gang was led by Michael Wade, a deserter from the Tenth Michigan Cavalry. Some of the other members were also Union deserters. Major Bingham led an attack against the desperadoes in May 1865, an attack that left dead two members of Bingham's command from Caldwell County. A couple of weeks later, a group of former Confederate soldiers set fire to the house and captured several of the robbers as they tried to escape. These men were summarily executed. In the Beaver Dam area, Alex Wilson had just returned from the war when he was arrested and taken to Tennessee, charged with the murder of Jack Potter. Wilson "was tried in some kind of court and sentenced to death." However, family members paid off the judge and other officials, and Wilson escaped. In February 1866, Keith Blalock caught up with John Boyd in Caldwell County, shooting and killing Boyd. Blalock was arrested for murder but was pardoned by Governor Holden before the trial. It was reported in May, "A large band of deserters, bushwhackers, robbers and disreputable characters generally have associated themselves into a regularly organized 'company' under the leadership of a notorious villain named Blalock, on John's River." The Blalocks soon left the county, heading to Texas.[116]

Often the question arises: how did these men who chose to remain in the area after the war react to loved ones who had fought on the other side? According to a history of the Banner Elk community, Frank Banner served on the Confederate side, while his brother Tatum Banner served on the Union side. They returned home within one hour of each other after the close of the war and "promptly got into a fight over which side was the aggressor." A memoir from the Sutherland community of Ashe County, just a mile from the Watauga County line, recorded that many of the boys of the Blue and Gray "found it rather hard to adjust themselves to this situation." Most of these encounters between family members who fought on opposing sides seem to have been forgotten.[117]

In August 1865, Holden called for a September election for delegates to an October meeting in Raleigh. Watauga's delegate to the convention was George W. Bradley, a merchant listed as living in the Blue Ridge district in 1860. The delegates repudiated the state's war debt, nullified the secession ordinance and abolished slavery; the Thirteenth Amendment to the United States Constitution was not passed until December 1865. Little is known about slaves in Watauga County during the war years. According to the comptroller's reports, there were 104 slaves in Watauga in 1860, 117 in 1862 and 125 in 1863. There was not a listing for 1864, so it is not possible to gauge accurately the effect of Lincoln's Emancipation Proclamation. Through family stories, we do know that several freed slaves chose to remain in the area. Lewis Banner bought land and gave it to his former slaves so they could live there after the war. Jacob Horton, a slave of John "Jack" Horton, continued to live with his former master for three years after the war had concluded. A slave named Done belonged to the Thomas and Ermine Farthing family. He continued to live with the widowed Ermine for some time before going to live with their daughter Polly until he died.[118]

In early 1866, several Federal officers were ordered to go into the western North Carolina counties to investigate alleged wrongs to former Union soldiers and sympathizers. Right after the war, Governor Holden had appointed Union sympathizers to local political offices. However, the election of late 1865 removed Holden and many of his appointees from office. In many cases, former Confederates gained those offices, and grand juries in some counties began to arrest Union supporters who had terrorized and plundered the mountain counties. It was so bad in Watauga County that the foreman of the grand jury told Lewis Banner that "a tory (meaning a Union man) need not come there for law—for he could not get it." It soon became clear to Congress that Presidential Reconstruction had failed, based on the election of late 1865; the set of "Black Codes" passed in January 1866 to maintain white supremacy; and the General Assembly's Amnesty Act of 1866, which pardoned civilian and military men for acts committed during the war but did not absolve civilians who served as guides or spies or had avoided conscription. In May 1867, Congress passed the first of its Reconstruction Acts, placing Southern states and their governors under the control of the military and demanding that the states draft new constitutions that had to be submitted to Congress for approval. These new state constitutions had to allow freedmen the right to vote, and the new General Assembly elected under the new constitution had to ratify the Fourteenth Amendment. Once these criteria were met, a state could be readmitted to the Union. On June 25, 1868, North Carolina was readmitted to the Union.[119]

Comparing the 1860 census to the 1870 census provides some small degree of insight into the cost of the war locally. In 1860, the eighteen slave owners in the county had real property valued at an average of $5,269 per person. Sixteen of those former slave owners found in the 1870 census had an average real property value of just $1,516. While this class held slightly more property in 1870, overall production was down for commodities like wheat, Indian corn and oats. Sheep held on farmsteads remained on par for 1860, but swine, the backbone of rural economy, fell drastically. The average number of swine per farm dropped from forty-five to seventeen.[120]

In 1889, Robert Farthing, speaking to Confederate veterans, believed that "the days of reconstruction" were "worse than the war if possible. We have now outlived it all, and we are truly thankful, and a better council and a better understanding now exist between the two sections and we believe the Union today is stronger than since the war. The soldiers, North and South, have brought this about more than politicians." Farthing believed that the old soldiers would have "arranged matters harmoniously" and that everyone would have been "better off than the war reconstruction did it." He believed this because the armies "contained the best men in the country and had sympathy for each other…they know how terrible was the war on both sides." That knowledge of just how terrible the war had been would remain with them for the rest of their lives.[121]

Chapter 8

Remembering Watauga County's Civil War

Across the state, the devastation wrought by the war, along with Reconstruction, discouraged large-scale commemoration and remembrance. Still, there were some localized acts, usually connected with the reburial of soldiers from plots on battlefields and near hospitals to more centrally located cemeteries. This relocation happened in Raleigh, Charlotte, Wilmington and Fayetteville. The first Confederate monument in North Carolina was dedicated on December 30, 1868, in Cross Creek Cemetery in Fayetteville. In Watauga County, there is no record of soldiers being reburied, although there are numerous accounts of the graves of lone soldiers buried where they died in locations throughout Watauga County.

The remembrance process in North Carolina truly began in October 1881, when a group of Confederate veterans, meeting at the state fair in Raleigh, formed the Confederate Survivors Association of North Carolina. Other states were forming groups as well; in 1889, representatives from these groups met in Louisiana and formed the United Confederate Veterans. The United Confederate Veterans was a fraternal organization. Each state constituted a division with its own elected leadership, while the division was made up of many different chapters, called camps. Each camp had a commander, lieutenant commander, adjutant, treasurer and, at times, a surgeon and a historian. Most camps met two or three times a year, usually on May 10, Confederate Memorial Day in North Carolina. The veterans often met and marched to the cemetery to clean and decorate the graves of their comrades who had passed on. Sometimes the veterans met in the fall for a picnic and then at some other point to elect new officers and to nominate comrades to attend the state and national reunions.

Local Confederate soldiers met at the courthouse in Boone in July 1889 and organized a Confederate Veterans Association. Captain Jordan Cook was elected chairman, and D.B. Dougherty was secretary. Robert Farthing was among the speakers that day, reminding those gathered that these former soldiers "still live representing to the world, bravery as soldiers in war, and in time of peace, true and noble citizenship." The first proposed reunion in Watauga County was scheduled to be held in Boone in October 1889. Participants came not only from Watauga but also from Caldwell and Mitchell counties, as well as Johnson County, Tennessee. The old veterans were organized into three companies. The first was composed of men who served in the Thirty-seventh Regiment and was placed under the command of Captain A.J. Critcher. A second company contained men who served in the Fifty-eighth Regiment and was placed under the command of Captains Benjamin Baird and William Hodges. A final company was composed of men who served in the First and Sixth Cavalry Regiments and was under the command of William Councill. Elected to command all three companies was Major G.W.F. Harper of Caldwell County. Harper apparently brought the surviving fragments of the flag of the Fifty-eighth Regiment with him, delighting many of the old soldiers. Many of the veterans spoke that day, and the reunion ended with Harper forming his battalion, marching the men through the streets of Boone and back to the courthouse and complimenting them on not forgetting the drill.[122]

There was much more talk in the newspaper about the 1890 reunion, this one held in Blowing Rock in August. The 1889 and 1890 reunions were unusual; not only were Confederate veterans invited but Federal veterans as well. The invitations went out far and wide. Former Federal general John Wilder, who owned Cloudland Hotel just across the Tennessee line, agreed to come. Confederate veteran and industrialist Julian S. Carr declined, saying he unfortunately would not be in the state at the time. Colonel George Folk planned to attend, as did Captain J.W. Todd of Ashe County. Local attendees were asked to bring "three days rations."[123]

Severe rains fell at the time of the 1890 reunion, and Major Harper did his best to call off the event. Nonetheless, a crowd of people arrived, and several speeches were made. These included opening remarks by Reverend Dr. Jethro Rumple and State Auditor G.W. Sanderlin. The next day, the weather had cleared, and a crowd estimated at two thousand had gathered. Colonel Folk addressed the crowd, followed by Reverend J.A. Weston.

Above: Although the photographer labeled this image "First March," is unclear if this image was in fact struck at the 1889 reunion in Blowing Rock or possibly in 1900 when the Nimrod Triplett Camp, United Confederate Veterans, was formed. *Author's collection.*

Left: Elijah Norris served in the Fifty-eighth North Carolina Troops and, for many years, as the commander of the Nimrod Triplett Camp of United Confederate Veterans. *Courtesy Wayne Brown.*

Others came and made short speeches; at the end of the day, the reunion was adjourned. "We think it was a great success, considering the adverse circumstances under which it was held," concluded the *Watauga Democrat.*[124]

In 1890, the U.S. Pension Office requested a special enumeration to help Union veterans locate those men with whom they had fought to testify in pension claims, while at the same time determining the number of surviving Union veterans and their widows. The enumerators were to count only Union veterans. There were sixty-two Union veterans living in Watauga County, with the highest concentration, eighteen men, living in the Cove Creek Township. The lowest concentrations were found in the Watauga and Blowing Rock Townships, with just two each. Neither of the two in Blowing Rock, James Teague and Charles Carter, are listed in the 1860 Watauga County census. They must have migrated to the area after the war. In the Shawneehaw Township, which contained Banner Elk, the most distinctly Unionist area of Watauga County, the enumerator counted not only Union but Confederate veterans as well. There were just ten Union veterans and nineteen Confederate veterans.[125]

Veteran reunions continued to occur with regularity into the 1890s. In 1891, the veterans met again in Blowing Rock, and the rain again hammered the participants on the first day of the reunion and on the afternoon of the second day. A band from Hickory provided the entertainment, and the veterans voted to move the reunion to Lenoir in 1892.[126]

The United Confederate Veterans held national reunions starting in 1889, and veterans from Watauga County often traveled to these events. Harvey Davis went to the reunion in Nashville, Tennessee, in June 1897. Davis found the weather "excessively hot" and the Tar Heel delegation "not so largely represented as some others of the States"; those Tar Heels participating in the grand march received the largest ovation and enthusiastic cheers. "When their three large silk banners hove in sight along the line of march with the words 'Tar Heels' in bright letters upon a red back ground, the crowds literally went wild," he chronicled in the paper. Davis also attended the 1899 reunion in Charleston, South Carolina, describing hundreds of his fellow Tar Heels in attendance, including some displaying North Carolina's distinct historic symbols. The old soldiers "on the parade with pine poles upon the end of which were hung a tar bucket, plainly marked 'Tar.' The hornet's nest, too, was in evidence." Davis reported seeing fellow members of the First Cavalry, Daniel Mast and Martin Moore, at the festivities in Charleston. In 1900, the delegates to the reunion in Louisville, Kentucky, included Harvey Davis, Elijah Norris, William Davis, Wesley Presnell and

Alfred Moretz. This same group, with the addition of Dr. J.M. Hogshead, attended the reunion in Memphis in 1901. The 1917 reunion was held in Washington, D.C., and J.W. Blair and T.H. Williams are reported to have attended as representatives of Watauga County. In 1919, Norris, Calvin Cottrell and J.W. Horton all attended the national reunion in Atlanta.[127]

A few of the veterans from the Fifty-eighth Regiment participated in marking the spot where they had fought in September 1863 during the battle of Chickamauga, Georgia. Brothers Benjamin and David Baird were a part of the committee. In the fall of 1893, David Baird and fellow veteran William S. Davis traveled to Chickamauga, examining the field and locating the area were they had fought. "They say the grounds," reported the *Watauga Democrat*, "are still natural and they had no trouble to locate the place occupied in the fight. They brought with them some relics from the battlefield." A marker to the Fifty-eighth Regiment was dedicated on the battlefield on November 10, 1905.[128]

"About 30 of the old Confederate Veterans met in the court house Tuesday and organized a company of Confederate Veterans," reported the *Watauga Democrat* on May 17, 1900. The new camp was christened the Nimrod Triplett Camp 1273. Triplett was a member of the First Cavalry, killed in action on July 10, 1863, on the retreat from Gettysburg. Captain Edward Lovill, a member of the Twenty-eighth North Carolina Troops who had moved to Boone after the war to practice law, was listed as the commander of the camp, while David Dugger (Thirty-seventh Regiment) was the adjutant. By 1905, Elijah Norris (Fifty-eighth Regiment) was listed as the commander of the camp. That year, the veterans held their reunion in the courthouse in Boone. Camp elections were held in the morning, followed by dinner, which the veterans apparently had brought themselves. "Under almost every shade tree might have been seen a clump of veterans and friends partaking of a sumptuous repast," reported the *Watauga Democrat.* Upon reassembly, the veterans took up the welfare of a comrade, Franklin Triplett, suffering with cancer. They raised eight dollars on the spot. At 3:00 p.m., the veterans formed into ranks and marched through the streets of Boone, singing "Dixie" and "Sallie Gooden." That evening, the veterans attended a service at the Baptist Church. The following day, they gathered again and listened to various speeches, agreeing in the end to hold the reunion the next year in Vilas.[129]

In 1901, the *Watauga Democrat* ran on the front page the new Confederate pension laws. In 1867, North Carolina had established its first pension act. Veterans who had lost an arm or leg could apply for a prosthetic limb or for reimbursement if they had privately purchased a prosthetic. Six Watauga

Erected in 1905, the monument to the Fifty-eighth North Carolina Troops is on Snodgrass Hill on the Chickamauga battlefield. *Author's collection.*

veterans—Smith Carroll, Robert Farthing, John Hicks, Michael Mitchell, Wesley Presnell and William Shull—applied. In 1885, North Carolina passed its first general pension act. Veterans who had lost a leg, eye or arm or who were incapacitated for manual labor were entitled to $30 annually. A widow whose husband was a soldier killed during the war and who had not remarried was also entitled to the same amount. However, a veteran or widow who owned property with a tax value more than $500 or who received a salary of more than $300 a year was not eligible. The law was amended in 1887, allowing the application of widows of soldiers who had died of disease while in service. Any person applying had to have his applications certified, witnessed and filed with the county commissioners, who then sent them to the state auditor for approval. There were nineteen Watauga widows and seventeen soldiers who applied between 1885 and 1901.[130]

The General Assembly rewrote the pension laws in 1901. Pensioners were divided into four classes. First-class pensioners were totally disabled. Second-class pensioners were men who had lost a leg above the knee or an arm above the elbow. In the third class were men who had lost a foot or leg below the knee or an arm below the elbow or had received a wound that made a limb useless. The fourth-class pensioners consisted of men who had lost an eye

Above: Many local veterans' reunions featured a march of surviving soldiers. *Author's collection.*

Left: William S. Cook, Fifty-eighth North Carolina Troops, proudly displays his Southern Cross of Honor on his jacket. *Author's collection.*

or were unfit for general labor, and widows. In 1901, first-class pensioners received seventy-two dollars per year; second class, sixty dollars per year; third class, forty-eight dollars per year; and fourth class, thirty dollars per year. The 1901 Pension Act was modified several times over the coming decades, including in 1927, when black men who had served as cooks in the Confederate army became eligible to receive a pension for their service. The *Watauga Democrat* reported that July 1, 1901, was Confederate Pension Day in Watauga County. Apparently, all of the applicants had to fill out new applications. "The noble old boys and the widows of those who wore the gray, were here from every part of the county, and so large was the number that the applications sent out by the state were exhausted before noon and the services of clerks were employed to write them." In 1902 in Watauga County, there was one first-class pensioner, James Love; one second-class pensioner, George Younce; six third-class pensioners; and forty-seven fourth-class pensioners. Added to this were thirty widows of Confederate soldiers. All told, there were eighty-five pensioners in 1902, up from forty in 1901 when the system was still operating under the old pension laws.[131]

There was much discussion in 1905 of erecting a monument to the local Confederate dead in Boone. "Now, if Caldwell and other counties can do this why not Watauga," was the question proposed by the newspaper. Robert Rivers, the editor of the *Watauga Democrat*, gave five dollars toward the monument and began spreading the word, talking to the old veterans and the ladies. "Let us be up and doing," encouraged Rivers. The first two decades of the twentieth century were the high point of Confederate monument dedications in North Carolina, with at least fifty monuments being erected in those two decades. A group known as the United Daughters of the Confederacy worked on most of these projects. Watauga County, it appears, never had its own chapter of this organization, and the work was conducted by the veterans themselves. By the October 1905 reunion, a committee was established with Captain Lovell as chairman, William C. Coffey as treasurer and Rivers as secretary. Just why a monument was never actually erected in Boone remains unclear.[132]

Confederate veteran reunions continued with some regularity. In October 1907, sixty of the old veterans gathered on the grounds of the Appalachian Training School. Music was provided by the Walnut Grove Band, and speeches were delivered by Captain Todd of Jefferson and Captain Lovill, with a large dinner the next day. According to the newspaper, "The pathetic part of the meeting came when to the strains of 'When the roll is called up yonder,' they bade each other an affectionate farewell." In September 1908, the reunion was held at the Walnut Grove Academy. Jonathan Miller was appointed camp historian and undoubtedly began working on his book *Watauga Boys in the Great Civil War.* In September 1910, Boone hosted the reunion, which included a Masonic parade, a drum and fife corps, the Walnut Grove brass band and a few sons of Confederate Veterans mounted on horses. After the speeches ended, the "picnic grounds were thrown open, free to the dear old boys who wore the gray…The table was more than 150 feet in length, and laden with the very best that this favored country produces." Boone also held the 1911 reunion. Like the previous reunions, there were speeches, dinner and parades of the old veterans. Editor Rivers lamented that the roll call of veterans, "the most pathetic event of these annual gatherings, discloses the fact that 8 of the old men who had answered their names from year to year had met the Conqueror since the last meeting, and only 55 members of Camp Nimrod Triplett, answered their names."[133]

There were actually more than just 55 surviving Confederate veterans in Watauga County at the time. According to the 1910 Watauga County census, there were a total of 170 veterans still alive in Watauga County. Of those, 139 were Confederate veterans, and 31 were Union veterans.

Watauga County's veterans made a rare political statement in 1912, passing a resolution asking the state to repeal a law that stated that widows had to be married prior to 1869 to qualify for pensions. The Watauga veterans believed that the date should be set at 1880. Furthermore, they asked for the current "pauper pension law" to be replaced by an "Honor Roll Pension Law." Finally, the Watauga veterans asked that the amount paid to veterans be increased, and that instead of once a year, the funds should be distributed quarterly.[134]

Reunion attendance continued to decline. At the two-day reunion in August 1915, there were thirty-four veterans present the first day and forty-one the following day. The schedule of events in 1915 was generally the same one used for most years. The meeting was called to order by camp commander Elijah Norris. Devotional exercises were conducted by L.D. Cole, following the welcoming address by Calvin Cottrell, "one of the oldest veterans of Boone." The Reverend E.M. Gragg then addressed the crowd. This was followed by dinner, and at 1:30, Norris called the meeting back to order. J.F. Spainhour addressed the group, with "talks by several veterans" coming next. Norris adjourned the meeting until 9:00 a.m. on Friday, when devotional exercises were again carried out by Cole. J.W. Holtsclaw then presented the report from the committee on obituaries, which was adopted. Next came the memorial exercises, conducted by L.W. Farthing. "Several of the veterans made talks of respect to the memory of their departed

An early 1900s reunion of Watauga County Veterans. *Back row, left to right:* Sam Bishop, Elijah Norris, William Blair, William P. Coffey, — Critcher, John Hodges, Harvey Davis, Bill Hodges, William S. Cook, Jerome Presnell and Bill Norris. *Front row:* unknown, unknown, Ranzey Miller, Henry Miller, Wiley Norris, unknown, — Farthing, unknown, Calvin Cotrell, unknown, Webster Davis and Speck Henson. *Courtesy Mike Hartley.*

comrades"; those deceased comrades included Jonathan Miller, J.H. Brown, Timothy Moretz, D.B. Wagner, James Winkler, John Greenfield, James Crisenberg and James Conley. A vote was then held on officers for the next year, with the same slate being elected, save for the position of sergeant major, with J.W. Holtsclaw being elected to fill in for the deceased Brown. J.M. Payne then addressed the crowd before adjourning for dinner. Once again called to order by Norris, the veterans listened to drum and fife music before being addressed by distinguished state historian Frederick Olds. Norris then adjourned the meeting until the following year.[135]

Olds addressed the veterans again in 1917, when the reunion was held at Henson's Chapel in the Cove Creek area. The old veterans declared this reunion, "The greatest time ever!" There were forty-one veterans present. After business was concluded on Thursday, the veterans assembled around campfires and told "stories of the 'Sixties." The highlight of this reunion was an address entitled "Soldiers of North Carolina," by Miss Anna Smith, the granddaughter of Abner Smith, killed in March 1862. The reunion in 1922 was held at the Appalachian Training School. "These old veterans," reported the newspaper, "seemed to enjoy most fully their stay, as the school authorities were no less glad to have them."[136]

In 1927, a debate arose over who was the oldest Confederate veteran still alive in the state. As the dust settled in the debate, it was decided that Watauga County's Albert Wilson, at the age of 102, was the oldest. Wilson joined Company E, Thirty-seventh Regiment in September 1861 at the age of 33. He was promoted to first sergeant before providing a substitute and being discharged in February 1862. Wilson did not live to see his 103rd birthday, passing away on February 4, 1928.[137]

"South's Soldiers Feted as the Last Reunion is Held," read the *Watauga Democrat* on October 2, 1930. Seven veterans were at the reunion held on the grounds of the Appalachian State Teachers College. "Although their stride was faltering, their shoulders stooped by the weight of passing years, and their old eyes dimmed by the ever-changing scenes of long lifetime," recorded the newspaper, "these battle-scarred 'Rebels' who fought so valiantly under the Southern Cross seemed to be imbued with the zest of young manhood as they swapped yarns with each other, and felt so firmly cemented during that bloody conflict of the sixties." Those seven veterans present were Elijah Norris, William Spainhour, Harvey Davis, Tom Love, Marion Millsaps, Marshall Made and Wyatt Hayes. Speaking that day were Reverend P.A. Hicks, pastor of the First Baptist Church of Boone, and Professor A.M. Norton of the college, along with Dr. B.B. Dougherty. Norris was quoted as saying that the "curtain has fallen on the activities of Camp Nimrod Triplett. The simple memorial service was the finale."[138]

The old veterans were passing over the river. Often, their obituaries held clues to their service in the armies during the war. George W. Moody passed in November 1905, and the paper recorded his service in Company I, Fifty-eighth Regiment. Not long after volunteering, "his health failed him, and he was furloughed home and was not able to return any more." Former captain Joseph W. Todd passed in 1909. Following the war, he had moved to Ashe County to practice law. The community of Elks Cross Roads was renamed Todd in his honor. Todd was a central figure at many of the early veteran reunions. Calvin Cottrell, a member of the Fifty-eighth Regiment, passed in July 1923. He was considered the "Best Known Man in the Whole County of Watauga." Elijah Norris, a veteran of the Fifty-eighth Regiment and for years the commander of local United Confederate Veterans camp, answered the "Final Roll Call" in May 1933. Norris was eighty-nine years old.[139]

Albert P. Wilson (center) surrounded by other, unidentified Confederate veterans, at a very late reunion. *Courtesy Sandra Blankenship/Clinton Getzinger.*

Watauga County's last Confederate veteran did not pass until May 1946. J. Elihu Luther, at the age of 102, died at his home in Deep Gap. Luther lived in Wilkes County prior to the war and served in the Thirty-seventh Regiment. He moved to Watauga County later in life. Funeral services were conducted at the Gap Creek Baptist Church by the Reverend E.C. Hodges, and Luther was buried at Gap Creek Cemetery. This aged veteran left behind scores of descendants.[140]

Chapter 9

Wataugua County's Unionists

In 1862, in a pamphlet entitled "Alleghania: A Geographical and Statistical Memoir," James W. Taylor wrote, "In the Union camps of East Tennessee, there are numerous volunteers from Watauga and other adjacent counties over the border." Throughout the decades, others have faithfully followed this theme. When Shepherd M. Dugger penned his *War Trails of the Blue Ridge* in 1932, he wrote freely of all the Unionists who lived within one mile of him in the Banner Elk area. William Trotter, in his work *Bushwhackers*, claims that Watauga County was strongly Unionist throughout the entire war. In December 2010, Kevin Oshnock, in his master's thesis entitled "The Isolation Factor: Differing Loyalties in the Mountain Counties of Watauga and Buncombe During the Civil War," writes repeatedly of the strong Unionist sentiment in Watauga County, going so far as to state that "much of Watauga County remained Unionist with only a couple of districts showing strong Confederate support." Yet numbers produced by an examination of enlistment patterns and the census records show a very different story.[141]

It is not easy to produce solid records regarding enlistment data in Watauga County. The census takers in 1860 missed scores of families. Some family groups appeared on the 1850 census and the 1870 census, but they were overlooked in 1860. A few might have even been elsewhere. For example, Harvey Bingham, who commanded the home guard, was away at school when the census taker came calling. One tabulation of everyone claiming residence or enlistment in Watauga County shows a total of 793 men (and one woman) who joined the Confederate army. Of those men, 61 deserted the Confederate army and joined 50 other Watauga County men in the Union army. Added to this are 19 other men who stated that they served in the Confederate army (enlistment details are lacking), along with 108 men in the home guard and 23 militia officers, to produce a total of 898 enlistments in Watauga County. A second set of numbers comes from Terrell Garren's 2006 book, *Mountain Myth: Unionism in Western North Carolina.* In his research, Garren found a total of 936 men in Confederate service and only 47 in Union service. Yet a third set of numbers can be extracted from the 1860 census, based on the original survey. In the census, 530 men (and one woman) could be documented enlisting in the Confederate army. Of these, 41 deserted and joined with 36 more to serve in the Federal army. Of the home guard members, 116 can be documented. While these three sets of numbers vary, it does show one important aspect: the majority of men in Watauga County strongly supported the Confederacy.[142]

Oshnock claims that save for a couple of districts, "much of Watauga County remained Unionist." Scrutinizing the 1860 census shows otherwise.

District	CS Enlistment	CS/US	US Enlistment
Valle Crucis	58	4	2
Boone	75	—	—
Mtn. Home	2	—	9
Cove Creek	73	8	10
Meat Camp	75	1	—
Blue Ridge	103	17	9
Laurel Creek	37	7	2
Beaver Dam	45	4	4

The hardest district to decipher is the Mountain Home district. In early 1861, much of this district was severed from Watauga County and added to the newly created Mitchell County. The portion that remained, much of the Banner Elk area, was strongly pro-Union. Yet much of the southern portion of the Mountain Home district, the area around Altamont and Linville Falls in present-day Avery County, was strongly pro-Confederate. While the Banners and Von Cannons remained in Watauga County, deciding just where the split occurred in the census is nearly impossible.

The enlistment information for the area's Federal soldiers reveals that only the group containing the Banners enlisted in 1862. There were twenty-two men who enlisted in the Federal army in 1863, twenty-six in 1864 and six in 1865. But even some of these men were not truly Unionists. At least three Watauga County men—Hezekiah Thomas, Thomas Fletcher and John S. Farthing—were Confederate prisoners of war and, when given the chance, took the Oath of Allegiance to the Federal government and joined one of six United States volunteer regiments. These regiments were sent out west to battle the Native Americans. Hezekiah Thomas (Fifty-eighth Regiment) provides an interesting look into the conditions that prompted a few men to become "galvanizers," the term used for Confederates who joined the Federal army. Thomas was captured in September 1864 near Jonesboro, Georgia, and eventually landed at Camp Douglas in Chicago, Illinois. Thomas stated that he and "thousands more…were all about to starve to death," when a recruiter came through the camps and "thousands" of Confederates chose to join the other side. Thomas was mustered into the Sixth United States Volunteers and "taken out to Fort Kerney, in Nebraska(,) and from there I was taken to Grand Island (Nebraska) to make hay for the Government and while there some of the Government horses were stolen and…(I was detailed with a corporal) to go…hunt for the horses; so we followed the horses for about 400 miles, and after we got there we decided to come home and we never went back to get our discharge." An accurate account of just how many men had similar reasons for joining the Federal army remains unclear.[143]

It is also interesting to note that about half of the men who joined the Federal army waited until the Federals came to them. Keith Blalock hesitated until mid-1864 to join the Tenth Michigan Cavalry, stationed just across the Tennessee State line. Likewise, the men joining the Second and Third North Carolina Mounted Infantry (U.S.) were never far from home. These two regiments were stationed in east Tennessee or western North Carolina for the duration of the war. As is evident, many of them were seldom better than scoundrels and thieves, often roaming the mountains in small groups plundering and committing other depredations. However, those who joined the Thirteenth Tennessee Cavalry did see regular service, not only in Tennessee but also as far away as Salisbury, North Carolina. Unlike the Second and Third North Carolina Regiments, the Thirteenth Tennessee functioned as an actual regiment. At least three men—John Miller, William Hampton and Alfred Hilliard, all Confederate prisoners of war—joined the United States Navy.

James Hartley was an "underground railroad" pilot, guiding escaped Union prisoners and dissidents, and then later became a lieutenant in the Third North Carolina Mounted Infantry (U.S.). *Courtesy Sandra Pierson.*

In 2011, Dr. Joseph Glatthaar released a book examining six hundred soldiers who served under General Robert E. Lee in the Army of Northern Virginia. In his survey, he found the average soldier was born in July 1835. For Watauga County, the average soldier was born in April 1838: there were more Confederate soldiers born in 1838, or after, than prior to that year.[144]

Glatthaar goes on to break up his surveyed men into three groups. The poorer economic class had a combined personal and real property value from $0 to $799, based on the 1860 census. The middle class ranged from $800 to $3,999, while the wealthy class was worth more than $4,000. Glatthaar found that 79.1 percent of his survey soldiers were in the poorer class, 10.5 percent were in the middle class and 10.3 percent were in the upper class. In looking at 430 Watauga County men who joined the Confederate army (and did not desert and join the Federal army), 45.3 percent were from the poorer class, 47.4 percent were from the middle class and 7.2 percent were from the upper class. For those who first enlisted in the Confederate army, only to later desert and join the Federal army, 48.2 percent were from the poorer class, while 51.7 percent were from the middle class. None were from the upper class. Watauga County men who joined the Federal army came from the poorer and middle classes, 41.4 and 51.7 percent, respectively, with just 6.9 percent from the upper class.[145]

William H. Horton (Fifty-eighth Regiment) complained in a letter home in November 1864, "This cruel war is a rich man's war and a poor man's fight." That was a common cliché during the war and has resonated with scholars to this day. However, many found in Watauga County's upper-class bracket were deeply involved in the war. Of thirty-five Watauga County men with real and personal wealth above $4,000, eight served in the Confederate army, while eleven others were too old for active service and sent their son(s), who were living at home, to serve in the army. An additional four of these upper-class men served in the home guard.[146]

An untold story is that of the hundreds of men who simply refused to serve in either army, or enlisted in the Confederate army only to later desert and spend the rest of the war hiding out. In the Fifty-eighth Regiment as a whole, there were 707 confirmed deserters, yet only 135 men can be confirmed as joining the Federal army. Obviously they were not deserting to join the other side. The problem with trying to document these men is the lack of surviving records, coupled with the nuances of spelling of the day. It must suffice to say that there were men in Watauga County who cared neither for the Confederate government nor the Federal government. They simply wanted to be left alone.[147]

Many of the few slave owners in Watauga County supported the Confederacy. William F. Shull, Jonathan Horton, James W. Councill and George W. Folk all served, while the sons of Jesse Councill, Benjamin Councill, Phineas Horton, Alexander Green, Lot Estes and Reuben Farthing donned the gray. Likewise, home guard members Henry Taylor and John Norton also owned slaves. John "Jack" Horton, the outspoken Unionist who lost his houses in Boone to Kirk's men, had a son in the Confederate army. Another slave owner, David Lewis, had a son who first joined the Confederate army but later deserted and joined the Federal army. The prominent slave owner Lewis Banner sent all of his eligible sons to join the Federal army.

In some cases, the war was literally brother against brother. Jeremiah Green had three sons who served. His son Alfred enlisted in the Thirty-seventh Regiment in September 1861 but, after a stint in prison and a wound in 1864, he disappears from the regiment's records. Son Adam enlisted in the Fifty-eighth Regiment in July 1862. He died of unknown causes at a hospital in Clinton, Tennessee, on March 5, 1863. Son Isaac was conscripted into the Fifty-eighth Regiment in September 1862 and failed to return from a furlough. He appears after the war in the 1910 census as a Federal veteran.

These complexities of loyalty largely contributed to the painful and lingering effects of the conflict. The war was less physically destructive in Watauga County than in the battle-ravaged landscape of central Virginia and northwestern Georgia, but social, personal and emotional damage, impossible to calculate, was just as devastating. Families were torn asunder, homes and farms were destroyed and scores of men failed to return home at war's conclusion. In the end, it appears that there were at least 212 men from Watauga County who died as a result of the war. Of these, 58 were killed in combat or died of wounds, 152 died of disease or some type of accident and 2 were executed. At least 24 percent of Watauga County's soldiers died during the war.

Newton Greer was correct when he was recorded as saying, "You don't know anything about hard times unless you were in the Awful War." For the men and women who lived through the 1860s, that "Awful War" defined their lives, shaping both their personal stories and the story of this county. Though an often dark and grim one, the Civil War was a crucial chapter in the history of Watauga County.[148]

Appendix A

Looking for Watauga County's Civil War Soldiers Today

The men (and one woman) from Watauga County served in a variety of regiments during the war years. On the Confederate side, these included the Eleventh North Carolina Troops (also known as the Bethel Regiment), the Fourth North Carolina State Troops, the Twenty-sixth North Carolina Troops, the Thirty-second North Carolina Troops and the Twenty-first Virginia Cavalry. Of course, the majority of men served in the First North Carolina Cavalry, Thirty-seventh North Carolina Troops, Fifty-eighth North Carolina Troops and the Sixth North Carolina Cavalry. Likewise, local men joined a variety of Federal regiments. The majority served in the Third North Carolina Mounted Infantry and the Thirteenth Tennessee Cavalry, with a few men in the Second North Carolina Mounted Infantry, the Third Tennessee Mounted Infantry, the Fourth Tennessee Cavalry, the Fifth Ohio Infantry, the Sixth United States Volunteers, the Eighty-seventh Illinois Infantry and the United States Navy.

In looking for the service records for these soldiers, on the Confederate side, it is best to start with the *North Carolina Troops, 1861–1865,* eighteen volumes published by the North Carolina Division of Archives and History. Most North Carolina libraries have a set. From there, more information can be found on both Confederate and Union soldiers by requesting copies of their Compiled Service Records from the National Archives, or by subscribing to fold3.com or Ancestry.com. Pension records for Federal soldiers can be acquired from the National Archives. Pension records for Confederate soldiers can be found at the North Carolina Archives.

All of the primary regiments in which Watauga County men served have been chronicled in some form or fashion. These include Chris Hartley's *Stuart's Tarheels: James B. Gordon and His North Carolina Cavalry* (2011); Michael C. Hardy's *The Thirty-Seventh North Carolina Troops: Tar Heels in the Army of Northern Virginia* (2003); Hardy's *The Fifty-Eighth North Carolina Troops: Tar Heels in the Army of Tennessee* (2011); and Jeffrey Weaver's *The 5th and 7th Battalions North Carolina Cavalry and the 6th North Carolina Cavalry* (1995). Regimental histories on the Federal side include Matthew Bumgarner's *Kirk's Raiders: A Notorious Band of Scoundrels and Thieves* (2000) about the Second and Third North Carolina Mounted Infantry; Ron Killian's *A History of the Third North Carolina Mounted Infantry, U.S.A.* (2008); and the classic *History of the Thirteenth Regiment Tennessee Volunteer Cavalry, U.S.A,* (1903) by Samuel W. Scott and Samuel P. Angel, two veterans of that regiment.

Appendix B

The Song of the Home Guard

The Song of the Home Guard

(Composed about the Storys and other Union sympathizers who lived on the Blue Ridge in the Civil War days.)

Chorus: Sing, fal di dy do, fa di link a day
Sing, fal di dy do, fa di link a day

1. Old Johnie Story, a mighty man to brag,
Let his coat tail hanging on a snag. (Chorus)

2. Uncle Bill Cook, big man to be,
Indicted Old Reid for 'salt and batterie. (Chorus)

3. Old Joshua Story, he saw a little sight,
Which you may know he didn't much like. (Chorus)

4. Little Billie Benson, Johnsie's little son,
Got all excited and fled the wrath to come. (Chorus)

5. Old Walt Story like a half sided loon,
Made little progress on his way to Boone. (Chorus)

6. Uncle Aaron Hampton, whom you often see,
Going down the mountain to Aunt Betts McGee. (Chorus)

7. Aunt Susie Story, active as a spar',
Told all the boys she'd see them again tomor'. (Chorus)

8. Old Ginger Cake Story with his old goggle eyes,
Took more salt than you'd ever realize. (Chorus)

9. He went to the salt lick the Government to haul,
There ain't no devil if he didn't keep it all. (Chorus)

10. Here's little Jesse Peter with his little speckled horn,
He seemed mighty willing to acknowledge to the corn. (Chorus)

11. They asked Mrs. Hatten where Moody had gone,
Said she didn't know, he'd been gone so long. (Chorus)

12. She looked like satan, too mad to cry,
She wished they would take sore throat and die. (Chorus)[149]

Notes

DU: Duke University
NA: National Archives
NCSA: North Carolina State Archives
PC: Private collection, copy in author's possession
RG: Record group

Introduction

1. J.B. Miller, *The Watauga Boys in the Great Civil War.* (N.p., n.d.), 11.

Chapter 1

2. Daniel J. Whitener, *History of Watauga County* (Boone, NC: N.p., 1949), 43.
3. Michael C. Hardy, *A Short History of Old Watauga County.* (Boone, NC: Parkway Publishers, 2005), 47; James Boykin, *North Carolina in 1861* (New York: Bookman Associates, 1961), 84.
4. *Fayetteville Observer,* 13 August 1860.
5. William Powell, *North Carolina through Four Centuries* (Chapel Hill: University of North Carolina Press, 1989), 143.
6. John B. Palmer to Andrew Johnson, 25 August 1865, Case Files of Applications From Former Confederates for Presidential Pardons, 1861–1867, RG 94, NA; Raleigh *Register,* 13 March 1861; John McCormick,

Personnel of the Convention of 1861 (Chapel Hill: University of North Carolina Press, 1900), 18.
7. John Barrett, *North Carolina in the Civil War* (Chapel Hill: University of North Carolina Press, 1963), 10.
8. Military Records, Watauga County, NCSA.
9. Francis Dedmond, "Harvey Davis's Unpublished Civil War Diary," *Appalachian Journal* (Summer 1986: 368–407, 370, 379); Louis Manarin, et al., *North Carolina Troops,* 18 volumes (Raleigh: North Carolina Division of Archives and History, 1961–present), 2:36, 40, 42.
10. Dedmond, "Harvey Davis," 382; Hattie Green. Oral History Project Collection, No. 87. Appalachian Collection, Appalachian State University.
11. Noble J. Tolbert, ed., *The Papers of John Willis Ellis,* 2 volumes (Raleigh: North Carolina Department of Archives and History, 1964), 2:844–45; Holtsclaw to Adjutant General, 8 August 1861, Adjutant General's Papers, NCSA.
12. *Weekly Standard* (Raleigh), 17 July 1861.
13. Michael Hardy, *Thirty-Seventh North Carolina Troops* (Jefferson, NC: McFarland and Company Publishing, 2003), 12–14; *Watauga Democrat,* 27 January 1898; 3 February 1898.
14. *Raleigh Register,* 21 August 1861; *Catawba Express,* reprinted in *August Chronicle* (GA), 4 September 1861; *Raleigh Standard,* 14 September 1861; Barzilla McBride to brother and sister, 25 August 1862, PC.
15. *Springfield Republican* (MA) 19 Nov. 1861; *Boston Traveler* (MA) 18 Nov. 1861.
16. *North Carolina Standard,* 4 December 1861.

CHAPTER 2

17. Manarin, *North Carolina Troops,* 9:486, 524; Bennett Smith to Dear Wife, 17 April 1862, PC.
18. Michael Hardy, *Fifty-Eighth North Carolina Troops* (Jefferson, NC: McFarland and Company Publishing 2011), 28.
19. Ibid., 30.
20. *Watauga Democrat,* 15 September 1901.
21. Hardy, *Fifty-Eighth North Carolina,* 47–48.
22. Terry Harmon, *The Harmon Family, 1670–1989* (Boone, NC: Minor's Publishing Company, 1984), 57, 80; Sanna Gaffney, *Heritage of Watauga County, North Carolina, Volume 1* (Winston-Salem, NC: Hunter Publishing Company, 1984), 99.

23. Shepherd Dugger, *War Trails of the Blue Ridge* (Banner Elk, NC: n.p., 1932), 203; "The Banner Brothers of Co. B, 4th TN Cav (USA)," online. Accessed 15 February 2002.
24. Manarin, *North Carolina Troops,* 7:535; Arthur, *Watauga County,* 160; *Western Democrat,* 6 May 1862.
25. Stephen Bradley, *North Carolina Confederate Militia Officers Roster* (Wilmington, NC: Broadfoot Publishing, 1992), 266–67.
26. Adjutant General to Evans, 7 July 1862; Adjutant General to Wm. Horton, 1 August 1862; Adjutant General to Ward, 14 October 1862, Adjutant General letterbook, NCSA.
27. Adjutant General to Wm. Horton, 19 September 1862, Adjutant General letterbook, NCSA.
28. Adjutant General to Wm. Horton, 13 October 1862, Adjutant General letterbook, NCSA; Manarin, *North Carolina Troops,* 9:587, 526; Bradley, *North Carolina Confederate Militia Officer Roster,* 266.
29. Manarin, *North Carolina Troops,* 14:416; Gerald Cook, *The Last Tar Heel Militia, 1861–1865* (Winston-Salem: [n.p.] 1987), 30.
30. *North Carolina Standard* (Raleigh), 18 October 1864.

CHAPTER 3

31. *Weekly Standard* (Raleigh), 5 November 1862; John Arthur, *Western North Carolina* (Boone, NC: D.H. Morrison, 1914), 255.
32. *Weekly Standard* (Raleigh), 7 January 1863; Bud Altmayer, *A Family History of Watauga County* (Boone, NC: Minor's Printing Co., 1994), 12.
33. Rebecca Hyatt, *The Adams Family in America: 1766–1954* (n.p., 1954), 19–22.
34. Altmayer, *A Family History of Watauga County,* 130–31.
35. Bennett Smith to Dear Wife, 8 May 1863, PC; Manarin, *North Carolina Troops,* 9:524; Cook, *Last Tar Heel Militia,* 35.
36. Jos C. Norwood to My Dear Walter, 13 August 1863, Lenoir Family Papers, Southern Historical Collection; Arthur, *History of Watauga County,* 170; *Historical Encyclopedia of Illinois,* Volume 3 (Chicago: Munsell Publishing Co., 1912), 1275.
37. *Asheville News,* reprinted in the *Fayetteville Observer,* 1 October 1863.
38. Bennett Smith to Dear Jane, 17 May 1863, PC; Manarin, *North Carolina Troops,* 9:535.
39. Manarin, *North Carolina Troops,* 14:315; Hattie Lewis, et. al., *History of Cove Creek Baptist Church, 1799–1999* (Sugar Grove, NC: Cove Creek Baptist Church, 1999), 10.

40. Elisha Trivett papers, PC; Cook, *Last Tar Heel Militia*, 41.
41. Nathan Horton to Mary Councill, 20 February 1863, Councill Papers, DU.
42. 1860 United States Federal Census, Watauga County.

CHAPTER 4

43. Enoch Swift Letter, Military Collection, NCSA; William Burson, *A Race For Liberty* (Wellsville, OH: O.W.G. Foster, 1867), 103–04.
44. *Charlotte Observer*, 27 May 1928; "The Dark Days of the War. History as Told by a Letter Book," *Charlotte Observer*, 4 July 1897.
45. Roy Weaver, "The Civil War in Watauga County" (unpublished manuscript, Watauga County Public Library), 8; Arthur, *Watauga County*, 345; Dugger, *War Trails*, 117; Gaffney, *Heritage of Watauga County*, 229.
46. "North Carolina in the War: Stories from an Old Letter Book," *Charlotte Observer*, 27 April 1902; John Jones, Southern Claims Commission Approved Claims, 1871–1880, RG 217, NA; Cook, *The Last Tar Heel Militia*, 41, 59.
47. Sandra Ballard and Leila Weinstein, *Neighbor to Neighbor: A Memoir of Family, Community, and Civil War in Appalachian North Carolina* (Boone, NC: Center for Appalachian Studies, 2007), 82.
48. Arthur, *Watauga County*, 172–73.
49. Bradley, *North Carolina Confederate Militia Officers Roster*, 266; Arthur, *Watauga County*, 340.
50. Dugger, *War Trails of the Blue Ridge*, 204.
51. Terrell Garren, *Mountain Myth: Unionism in Western North Carolina* (Spartanburg, SC: Reprint Company, 2006), 67–68; Matthew Bumgarner, *Kirk's Raiders: A Notorious Band of Scoundrels and Thieves* (Hickory, NC: Piedmont Press, 2000), 144–60.
52. John Horton, Southern Claims Commission Approved Claims, 1871–1880, RG 217, NA; Dugger, *War Trails*, 111.
53. Arthur, *Watauga County*, 345.
54. Francis Hosmer, *Andersonville and Other Writings* (Loring and Axtell, 1896), 15–23.
55. Junius Browne, *Four Years in Secessia* (Hartford, CT: O.D. Case, 1865), 391–93.
56. *Fayetteville Observer*, 1 August 1864; *Weekly Standard*, 2 September 1863.
57. *North Carolina Standard*, 18 October 1864.
58. Roy Weaver, *Tales of Aho* (Boone, NC: n.p., n.d.), 4; Hyatt, *Adams Family*, 22; Ina Van Noppen, *Stoneman's Last Raid* (Boone, NC: n.p., 1961), 22–3; Arthur, *Watauga County*, 169; *The Abington Virginian*, 20 November 1863.

59. Dugger, *War Trails,* 113–17; Arthur, *Watauga County,* 174; *Weekly Standard,* 23 November 1864.
60. *Public Laws in North Carolina,* Adjourned Session (1865), 65.
61. Barrett, *Civil War in North Carolina,* 241.
62. Vaughn to Vance, 6 December 1864, *Papers of Vance,* reel 13.

Chapter 5

63. *Congressional Record,* Vol. 169, (1886), 169.
64. Arthur, *Watauga County,* 160–66.
65. Lloyd Bailey, *The Heritage of the Toe River Valley, Volume 8* (Marceline, MO: Walsworth Publishing, 2009), 51; Arthur, *Watauga County,* 166–67.
66. Arthur, *Watauga County*, 174–77, 283–84; Dugger, *War Trails,* 118–19.
67. Adjutant General to Cook, 13 February 1865; Adjutant General to McGuire, 13 February 1865; Adjutant General's letterbook, NCSA.
68. Dugger, *War Trails,* 124.
69. Cornelia Spencer, *The Last Ninety Days of the War in North Carolina* (New York: Watchman Publishing Co., 1866), 193; Arthur, *Watauga County,* 178.
70. Manarin, *North Carolina Troops*, 14:388; Arthur, *Watauga County,* 177; Spencer, *Ninety Days,* 193–94.
71. Arthur, *Watauga County,* 179; John Horton, Southern Claims Commission Approved Claims, 1871–1880. RG 217, NA.
72. Arthur, *Watauga County,* 177; Spencer, *Ninety Days,* 193–94; Van Noppen, *Stoneman's Last Raid,* 18.
73. William Vandyke, Southern Claims Commission Approved Claims, 1871–1880, RG 217, NA.
74. John Horton, Southern Claims Commission Approved Claims, 1871–1880, RG 217, National Archives; Arthur, *Watauga County,* 179; Barry Buxton, *A Village Tapestry: the History of Blowing Rock* (Boone, NC: Appalachian Consortium Press, 1989), 3.
75. Gaffney, *Watauga County Heritage,* 377; *Watauga Democrat,* 23 August 1979.
76. Gaffney, *Watauga County Heritage*, 118, 373; Altmayer, *A Family History,* 98–99; *Watauga Democrat,* 10 October 1974; Bea Wellborn, e-mail to author, 14 February 2013.
77. Barlow, *The Horton Family in Western North Carolina,* 53; Altmayer, *A Family History,* 63; Rittenhouse Baird, Joshua Winkler, William Vandyke and John

Horton, Southern Claims Commission Approved Claims, 1871–1880 RG 217, NA; *Watauga Democrat,* 30 December 1928.

78. Gaffney, *Watauga County Heritage,* 179.
79. Arthur, *Watauga County,* 181; Ballard, *Neighbor to Neighbor,* 94–95.
80. *Charlotte Observer,* 22 December 1895; *Lenoir Topic,* 17 December 1890–14 January 1891; Spencer, *Last Ninety Days,* 195.
81. I. Harding Hughes, *Valle Crucis* (n.p., 1995), 67; Gaffney, *Heritage of Watauga County,* 89, 152, 2:40; Hyatt, *Adams Family,* 20.
82. Hyatt, *Adams Family,* 20.
83. Miller, *Watauga Boys*, 13.

Chapter 6

84. Gaffney, *Heritage of Watauga County*, 214.
85. Dedmond, "Harvey Davis," 379; Miller, *Watauga Boys,* 14.
86. Jonathan Horton, Compiled Service Record, RG 109, NA; Manarin, *North Carolina Troops,* 9:485, 523, 7:535, 2:42.
87. Bell Wiley, *Life of Johnny Reb* (Baton Rouge: Louisiana State University Press, 1943), 29; *Watauga Democrat,* 18 June 1891.
88. Undated newspaper article, local history files, Caldwell County Public Library.
89. Daniel Carlton diary, PC.
90. Manarin, *North Carolina Troops,* 2:37, 9:526, 14:320; Gaffney, *Watauga County Heritage*, 253.
91. Manarin, *North Carolina Troops,* 14:389, 9:495; undated newspaper clipping, *Watauga Democrat*, PC.
92. Gaffney, *Watauga County Heritage*, 238, 302.
93. "An Appeal For the Sick and Wounded Soldiers." Salisbury Hospital Committee.
94. B.C. McBride to parents, 15 November 1861, 13 December 1862, PC; James Tugman to parents, 10 February 1862, PC; Gaffney, *Heritage of Watauga County,* 16; Miller, *Watauga Boys,* 4.
95. Greg Mast, *State Troops and Volunteers* (Raleigh: North Carolina Department of Archives and History, 1995), 24.
96. Manarin, *North Carolina Troops,* 9: 494, 535; 14:319, 393, 419.
97. McBride to Dear Uncle, 26 July 1862, PC.
98. Miller, *Watauga Boys*, 4; Carlton dairy, PC; Dedmond, "Harvey Davis," 383–4.

99. Tugman letters, family files, Appalachian State University; Carlton diary, PC.
100. Silas Green to family, 5 January 1862, PC.
101. B.C. McBride to Mary Councill, 25 August 1861, 31 May 1863, Councill Papers, DU; Smith to Dear Wife, 6 March 1862, PC.
102. Smith to Dear Wife, 6 March 1862, PC; Green to family, 5 June 1862; Miller, *Watauga Boys*, 10; Weaver, *Tales of Old Aho*, 7; Smith to Dear Jane, 30 March 1862, PC; J.S. Councill to Mary Councill, Councill Letters, 4 February 1862, DU.
103. Dedmond, "Harvey Davis," 388; J.W. Dugger and William Thomas, "A Diary Kept by J.W. Dugger and William Thomas While in the Confederate Service, and Members of the 58th N.C. Regiment," transcribed from the *Watauga Democrat*, 11, 12; Gaffney, *Watauga County Heritage*, 213.
104. W.H. Horton to Mary Horton, 14 October 1864, 30 November 1864; J.W. Horton to Mary Councill, 20 July 1864, Councill Papers, DU; Dedmond, "Harvey Davis Diary," 394.
105. Smith to Dear Companion, 24 March 1863, PC.
106. Tugman to family, no date, Appalachian Collection; W.H. Horton to Mary Councill, 14 October 1864; J.S. Councill to Mary Councill, 17 January 1862, Councill Papers, DU; Silas Green to Dear Uncle, 5 January 1862; B.C. McBride to Aunt and Uncle, 15 September 1861, PC; Bennett Smith to Jane, 26 February 1863, PC; Hyatt, *Adams Family*, 18.
107. Bennett Smith to Dear Jane, 24 February 1862, PC.
108. Wiley, *The Life of Johnny Reb*, 159; Horton to Mary Councill, 23 October 1862, Councill Papers, DU.
109. Smith to Dear Jane, 30 March 1862, PC; Gaffney, *Watauga County Heritage*, 214.
110. *Regulations for the Army of the Confederate States* (Richmond, VA: J.W. Randolph, 1863), 407, 410; McBride to Uncle, 15 September 1861; J.S. Councill to Mary Councill, 17 January 1864, Councill letters, DU.
111. Manarin, *North Carolina Troops*, 2:39, 9:490; Jack Bunch, *Roster of Court Martials in the Confederate States Armies* (Shippensburg, PA: White Mane Books, 2000), 262; Hardy, *Fifty-Eighth North Carolina*, 107–8.
112. Carlton diary, 4; Bennett Smith to Dear Wife, 6 March 1862, PC.
113. Dedmond, "Harvey Davis," 285; Green to Eggers, n.d., Dickerson Collection; McBride to Uncle, 15 September 1861, PC.

Chapter 7

114. *Lenoir Topic,* March 1929.
115. Russell Koontz, *North Carolina Petition for Presidential Pardons, 1865–1868* (Raleigh: Friends of the Archives, 1996), 54; *Western Democrat,* 29 May 1866.
116. Arthur, *Watauga County,* 184; Ballard, *Neighbor to Neighbor,* 118–19; *Western Democrat,* 29 May 1866.
117. Elsie Beasley, *Photographs: Banner's Elk, North Carolina* (Sabre Printers, 2006), 36; Ballard, *Neighbor to Neighbor,* 127.
118. Beasley, *Photographs,* 12; John Horton, Southern Claims Commission Approved Claims, 1871–1880, RG 217, NA; "Farthing Heritage," 8.
119. E.A. Carr to J.A. Campbell, and Frank Wolcott to J.A Campbell, 18 July 1866, Jonathan Worth Papers, Governor's Papers, NCSA.
120. Altmayer, *A Family History,* 138–39.
121. *Watauga Democrat,* 11 July 1889.

Chapter 8

122. *Watauga Democrat,* 11 July 1889, 17 October 1889.
123. Ibid., 10 October 1889; 3 July 1890; 10 July 1890.
124. Ibid., 28 August 1890.
125. Sandra Almasy, *North Carolina 1890 Civil War Veterans Census* (Joliet, IL: Kensington Glen Publishing, 1990), 224–30.
126. *Watauga Democrat,* 27 August 1891.
127. Ibid., 8 July 1897; 25 May 1899; 17 May 1900; 16 May 1901; 15 October 1919; *Charlotte Observer,* 7 June 1917.
128. Hardy, *Fifty-Eighth North Carolina,* 179.
129. *Confederate Veteran* 9:7 (July 1901); *Watauga Democrat,* 17 May 1900; 1 June 1905, 5 October 1905.
130. Ashley Wagner, *Phantom Pain: North Carolina's Artificial Limbs Program for Confederate Veterans* (Raleigh: North Carolina Department of Cultural Resources, 2004), 44–250.
131. *Watauga Democrat,* 4 July 1901; *Watauga Ancestry,* (June 1997), 13–15.
132. *Watauga Democrat,* 6 June 1905; 5 October 1905.
133. *Watauga Democrat,* 3 October 1907; 24 September 1908; 15 September 1910; 5 October 1911.
134. Ibid., 3 October 1912.

135. Ibid., 12 August 1915.
136. *Watauga Democrat,* 16 August 1917; *Charlotte Observer,* 14 September 1922.
137. *Winston-Salem Journal,* 7 January 1928.
138. *Watauga Democrat,* 2 October 1930.
139. Ibid., 5 November 1908; 11 February 1909; *Winston-Salem Journal,* 10 July 1923.
140. *Watauga Democrat,* 9 May 1946.

CHAPTER 9

141. James Taylor, "Alleghania: a Geographical and Statistical Memoir" (Saint Paul, MN: Davenport, 1862), 14; Dugger, *War Trails,* 204; Kevin Oshnock, "The Isolation Factor: Differing Loyalties in the Mountain Counties of Watauga and Buncombe During the Civil War" (unpublished master's thesis, Appalachian State University, 2010), 37.
142. Garren, *Mountain Myth,* 20, 89.
143. Manarin, *North Carolina Troops,* 15:322.
144. Joseph Glatthaar, *Soldiers in the Army of Northern Virginia* (Chapel Hill: University of North Carolina Press, 2011), 3.
145. Ibid., 8.
146. W.H. Horton to Mary Horton, 30 November 1864, DU.
147. Hardy, *Fifty-Eighth North Carolina,* 186.
148. Gaffney, *Heritage of Watauga County,* 214.

APPENDIX B

149. Story family files, Appalachian Collection, Appalachian State University.

Index

About the Author

Michael C. Hardy's extensive scholarship into North Carolina and Civil War history has produced an array of articles, blog posts, and books, including *North Carolina Remembers Chancellorsville* (2013), *Civil War Charlotte: Last Capital of the Confederacy* (2012), *North Carolina in the Civil War* (2011), *The Fifty-eighth North Carolina Troops* (2011), *Remembering North Carolina's Confederates* (2006), *The Battle of Hanover Court House* (2006), *A Short History of Watauga County* (2005), and the *Thirty-seventh North Carolina Troops* (2003). He has been collecting information on Watauga County and her soldiers for eighteen years. *Watauga County and the Civil War* is his eighteenth book. He travels extensively as a speaker and is part of the North Carolina Humanities Council Road Scholars Program. In 2010, Michael was selected as Historian of the Year by the North Carolina Society of Historians. In addition to writing and researching, he enjoys traveling, hiking, and photography. He and his family live on the side of a mountain in what was once Watauga County.